RESULTS ON TARGET

RESULTS ON TARGET

PRACTICAL STEPS
to
IMPROVE RESULTS
and
AVOID TRAPS

BRUCE DILLMAN

OUTCOME PUBLICATIONS
Kansas City • Cincinnati • Palo Alto

To Brian

RESULTS ON TARGET

Copyright ©1989 by Bruce Dillman
All rights reserved. Reproduction or use of editorial or pictorial content in any manner without express permission is prohibited.

Published By
Outcomes Incorporated
7400 State Line, Suite 105
Shawnee Mission, Kansas 66208

Library of Congress Catalog Card Number 87-63384

ISBN: 0-944112-12-9

Manufactured in the United States of America

3 5 7 9 8 4 2

CONTENTS

Part 1 • Background	**5**
Introduction	5
1 – It's Easy to Get Results	9
2 – Your Master Key	12
Part 2 • Target on Results	**17**
3 – Think of a Result You Want	20
4 – Aim for a Positive Result	28
5 – Refine the Details	34
6 – Get Into It	40
7 – Expand Your Team	47
8 – Turn to Key Clues	61
Part 3 • Results on Target	**77**
9 – Recognize and Avoid Traps	80
10 – Establish Resourceful Attitudes	108
11 – Support with Mutual Trust	118
12 – Use Your Clues	129
13 – Loosen Up for Another Approach	133
14 – Take Yes for an Answer	142
15 – Step This Way	146
Part 4 • Parting Shots	**149**
16 – Target Practice	150
17 – Handling Manipulation	157
18 – In Conclusion	163
Sources	166
Index	169

ACKNOWLEDGEMENTS

Several people took time to read a manuscript of this book and contributed to its improvement: Michael Eric Bennett, David Brady, Bill Breyfogle, Crawford Clark, Bill Conboy, Sue Dillman, Susette Haden Elgin, Debbie Gardner, Mark Knapp, David Landis, Bill Oliver and Jill Pinkleman. Eric Davies, Robert Dillman, Al Hyer, Bob Leavitt, and Dave Polson provided timely technical support. Jim Treat provided technical and moral support beyond the call of duty. Sammye Henry did all of the above and also gave invaluable editorial service. Brian Dillman and Mike Gardner inspired this project through their encouragement and their superb demonstrations of the attitudes and techniques discussed in this book.

Words cannot adequately express my gratitude to these people. Thank you is a start. Thank you.

> Destiny is not a matter of chance,
> it is a matter of choice; it is
> not a thing to be waited for,
> it is a thing to be achieved.
> *William Jennings Bryan*

> Before I start my speech I'd
> like to say something.
> *Unknown Speaker*

INTRODUCTION

People across America have read and heard about Police Sergeant Michael Gardner. Magazines, newspapers, and television programs told how Gardner and his partner, Michael Broering, resolved conflicts peacefully to prevents violence and injury. The media focused on the fact that the two officers used humorous behavior to defuse dangerous situations.

But there's more to the Gardner story. In July of 1983 Mike saw nothing humorous about law enforcement, or life in general. He described the situation this way:

> After about six years of police work, I was starting to get stuck in a negative loop. I didn't want much to do with anyone when I was off duty. I was starting to think there were only two kinds of people in this world: cops and bad guys. A job I started out feeling very, very proud of, I was now dreading to go to every day.

Just one month later that same Michael Gardner enjoyed his work. It was interesting and worthwhile, and he was more effective than ever. In that month Mike found ways to use his talents and abilities more effectively. Now he has more control in key situations, and he gets results he wants more often.

To get results you want, more often, more systematically, more effectively—that's what this book is about. If you always get everything you want, you don't need this information. Most of us, though, would like to improve our personal or business results, but we are doing the best we know how now. If we knew how, we would do better. That's how I felt. That's how Mike Gardner felt. That's how many others felt.

One result I want is for you to realize you can keep your own personality and lifestyle (if you want to) and still improve many areas of your life. You already have the tools you need. Once you realize those things, you can apply the ideas on these pages as Michael Gardner and many others do to improve your attitudes, performance, and results.

Day after day people fall into traps without realizing it, then wonder why they don't get where they want to go. They may work hard to reach a goal, then realize they don't want it. Sometimes people get what they want and don't know how; sometimes they get what they don't want and don't know why. Often they just don't know what they want.

When I was in that plight—wondering what happened and, wishing I could get results consistently ON TARGET—even one or two of these ideas would have helped a great deal.

When I first operated a personal computer, I had little instruction. Manuals were not much help. They did not relate to any language or experience I was familiar with. I did get the results I wanted from the computer by trial and error—and error. Later I wrote a manual for people who had never touched a computer, and that was the book I wished I'd had to start with.

Results On Target is the book I wish I'd had when I first wondered how to improve the results I got.

Credit is Due

In the computer book, I interpreted information from various sources and arranged it in a way I found useful. The basic processes had been in use for some time, and they were usually obvious—right after someone else pointed them out to me.

Results On Target is like that. In this case John Grinder, Richard Bandler, and associates of theirs did most of the pointing. With their models of human behavior Grinder and Bandler put together a program which is usable, useful, efficient and effective for getting things done. This book consists of my interpretation of a portion of that program supplemented and illustrated from sources such as Stafford Beer, Arthur Conan Doyle, Edward T. Hall, S. I. Hayakawa, Mark L. Knapp, Robert H. McKim, and others. My practical experience was greatly enhanced when Genie Z. Laborde gave me an extraordinary opportunity to find out how this stuff really works. Nothing here is intended to imply that any of these people endorses this interpretation—or would even recognize it if they heard it.

Working Hard, or Working Smart?

Although working hard has long been considered a virtue—especially by those who pay for it—*working smart* is usually more productive. People can work hard tilling the soil with sharp sticks, but in most cases they can do it better and faster with a tractor and plow. People can figure out mathematical equations, but computers do it faster and more accurately. So the person who works smart uses the available information and technology—when it is appropriate—and improves the results.

Buildings don't grow wild. Each one starts as somebody's idea. Architects turn vague, rough ideas into detailed drawings, models, and blueprints. Then other skilled people turn those blueprints into buildings.

Part 1 lays a foundation. In Part 2 we Target On Results by taking rough ideas and turning them into detailed models or TARGETS. Part 3 discusses ways to improve your ability to turn those models into concrete results—RESULTS ON TARGET.

None of these steps is useful to people stuck in quicksand, caught in a snare, or laid up from shooting themselves in the foot. Part 3 discusses recognizing and avoiding traps— major steps toward reaching any TARGET.

Avoiding unnecessary trouble makes sense. Using resources efficiently and effectively makes sense. Going for something you really want—on purpose and with confidence that you can get it—makes sense. Understanding and using the ideas on the following pages can help you do those things.

Beneficial Tools

These ideas can be extremely useful for attaining almost any result you might want—at home, at work, at play, or anywhere else. You can follow the procedure as it is laid out, or you can tailor the ideas to your own needs. Either way you will have a set of effective tools custom-made for your own special TARGETS.

But even beneficial tools—including these—can do harm unless people use them responsibly. The tools presented here work best when used for the benefit of everyone involved, but some people do not realize that. There are people who use some of these tools—accidentally or on purpose—to take advantage of others. By knowing how the steps work you can defend yourself from that kind of manipulation. Chapter 17 has more thoughts on manipulation, ethics, and self-defense.

Speaking of ethics, this is a good place for the guarantee.

LIMITED WARRANTY

The information in this book is accurate to the best of our knowledge. All recommendations are made without any guarantees from Outcome Publications. The author and publisher disclaim all liability in connection with the use of this information.

That legal talk means the material in this book can help improve your ability to get wanted results, *when you use it appropriately*. But neither the author nor the publisher has any control over how much of the information you read, how you remember it, or how you use it, so we cannot be responsible for the quality of your results. However, we will guarantee this: *the steps will* not *work if you do* not *use them.*

WARNING

- Many of the ideas you will read in the book may seem simple. Some are. Nobody said it had to be difficult.
- Some things seem so obvious they go without saying. Remember the obvious. Things that go without saying are often overlooked.
- Some of the material may be familiar. That is expected. It is like going to a class reunion where you meet people you remember, people you forgot, and people you never met. The important thing is that they are together now.
- The ideas are too important to take seriously. The jokes, acronyms, and other devices are to get your attention, clarify ideas, aid your memory, and lighten up the process.
- Some things, which may look like lists, are set that way to clarify, highlight, or organize ideas. Do not memorize them —unless you want to.
- Here is the procedure: I'll tell you the process. You decide when and how to use it. Use any or all steps, in order or not. Use whatever you think will get the results you want.
- Theoretically, using these steps long enough will get results you want in any situation, Actually, you may want to limit the time and effort you put into less-promising prospects.
- You have everything you need to use the steps, but to find out how they work for you, you must use them yourself.
- We can't expect any process to work with everybody, or to work with one person all the time. Most things suggested here have exceptions. Chapter 13 deals with exceptions.

> I want results!
> *Many Executives*

> A lot of people try.
> You succeed.
> *Rick Blaine*

1
IT'S EASY TO GET RESULTS

Now for an idea whose time has come—Random Air Lines.

    Random is a proposed super-efficient air line which will give the traveling public the features it wants most—fine service, extra-low fares, on-time flights, easy check-in, and no hassles. The idea is so simple it is surprising no one else has thought of it.

TAKE THE EASY WAY
RANDOM AIR
ANYWHERE

- *Low Fares*
- *Comfort*
- *Convenience*
- *Service*

- *No Restrictions*
- *No Delays*
- *No Worry*
- *No Hassle*

**Just come to the boarding gate when you're ready
RANDOM ... the air line whose time has come!**

When Random Air is in operation its passengers will just show up at the airport the day they want to travel, check their baggage at the curb, proceed directly to the gate, and immediately board the plane. They will buy their tickets on the plane, which takes off as soon as it is full.

Think of the advantages for passengers and for stockholders. The company will have no expense for reservation and ticketing facilities, and every flight will be full. Passengers will have no inconvenience from overbooking, nasty ticket agents, cancelled flights, or long waits in airports.

The only possible drawback is that passengers have no choice of destination. But they will arrive somewhere, and fares are so low that if they don't like that place, they can get right back on a plane and go somewhere else. Even those with a particular destination in mind will eventually get there, if they take enough planes. And they may like one of their stops even better than where they originally thought they wanted to go.

It should fly. Soon people will be saying, "I go the Random way." Why not? This is a time-honored way of doing things. Many of us already take the Random way in other situations. We do what we usually do, we take what comes, and then we decide whether we like it or not.

We go Random for good reasons.

- It is easy.
- It is a habit.
- We often do not know what we really want.
- Sometimes it works.
- We don't know a better way

There is nothing wrong with the Random way—unless you want specific results.

I Get Results!

The highest praise some people can give is "He (or she) gets results." With this book, you, too, can get results. You can also get results without the book. You can't avoid getting results. But what kind? **The idea is to get results you want.**

Ty Cobb got results. He had the highest lifetime batting average in major league baseball history, .367. that means for every 1000 times at bat, Cobb got 367 base hits. But what about the other 633 times at bat? He got results then, too. He got some kind of result every time he came to the plate. In fact, his results average was 1.000. But that included 633 results he didn't want.

Everything we do gets results. They may be intentional or accidental, wanted or unwanted. We may do something and we may do nothing. Still we get results. Pay the telephone bill and you can make phone calls. Don't pay it and you can't. Either way you get a result.

Although we cannot avoid getting results, few of us consistently get results we want. We realize we can do some simple things and pretty much control the outcome. Flip a switch and a light comes on. Squeeze a toothpaste tube and toothpaste comes out. But results of a more complex nature seem like buying a lottery ticket. We do the usual things and hope something good happens. That is the Random way.

The TARGET Way

The Random way works pretty well, but from time to time you may want something more reliable. To get a specific result, however, you need something specific to aim for. You need something in mind before you start out. You need a TARGET.

For getting more control of your results, the TARGET way has some advantages over the Random way.

- It is just as easy to use, when you know how.
- It, too, can become a habit.
- It aims you toward what you really want.
- It improves your chances of getting it.
- It is a better way.

We always get results. We have no choice about that. But we do have a choice about the kind of results we get. We can take steps to control the results we get, or we can go the Random way by default.

> Everything should be as simple
> as possible, but not simpler
> *Albert Einstein*

> We believe the way to success is
> by mastering the fundamentals.
> *Raytheon Commercial*

2
YOUR MASTER KEY

Harry Houdini on master keys:

> Such keys are made for opening a set or series of locks each of which has a different make of key so that one key will not open another lock in the set, yet, the holder of the master key will open all.

Reading is a master key to books, magazines, road signs and any other written matter. Seeing is a master key to reading. The master key to results is even more fundamental.

The Master Key to Results

You have plenty of experience getting results. Have you noticed how you get those results? Although you can find it in many forms, there is one way to get results. *We get results by sending and receiving messages* — a process known as communicating.

Nations send messages to nations. Companies send messages to companies. People send messages to other people and even to themselves. Our health depends on how effectively our cells send messages to each other. The process of sending and receiving messages is essential to maintaining life and pursuing happiness. *Everything we do is a result of communicating,* and *everything we do sends messages which get results.*

The way we communicate affects the results we get.

We send messages to workers to increase or decrease production. We send messages to customers to increase sales. We send a message to a waitress to order dinner. We receive messages from teachers to find out how, and what, kids do in school. We receive messages from our eyelids to go to sleep. A batter receives messages from the pitcher and sends messages to his muscles about where, when, and how to swing the bat.

The batter has less than half a second ("one thou−") to see a pitch, decide whether to swing, get his body in motion, and guide the bat to meet the ball. Control centers in his brain receive messages about the ball's speed and direction, compute where it will be in another fraction of a second, and send messages to activate certain muscles. It happens too fast to think about; it seems to happen automatically. Much of our sending and receiving is just as fast and just as automatic.

We are aware of some of our communicating, and we are unaware of most of it. We can communicate intentionally to get specific results, or we can do it unintentionally and get random results. We do a large share of our sending and receiving through force of habit while thinking about other things. This great labor-saving device can lead us to results we like. It can also lead us into traps and to results we don't like.

No 'Lack of Communication'

In a 1986 football game, an instant-replay official in the press box radioed to the referee on the field, "Pass *in*complete," and the referee announced to the world, "Pass *is* complete. Touchdown." A National Football League spokesman called it a "breakdown in communication." Managers say, "We need communication." People talk of husbands, wives, or children who "won't communicate." In *Cool Hand Luke* Strother Martin said, "What we have here is a failure to communicate."

Failure to communicate is impossible. No one has the luxury of choosing whether to communicate or not. Everybody is always sending messages, a lot of messages.

Silence can be a strong message. The letter that does not arrive can result in deep disappointment or the loss of a sale. A pause can have powerful meaning. The replay official communicated, even though his meaning was garbled and the result was not what he intended. That sort of thing happens often.

When people talk of failing to communicate, they probably mean they do not like the results they get. There is plenty of communicating, but it is not producing the results they want.

The Basics
- Everything we do gets some kind of result.
- Everything we do sends some kind of message.
- Everything we do is a result of communicating.
- We get results by sending and receiving messages.

To Get Results You Want

The processes for getting results you want are the same ones you used to get results you didn't want. You have a great deal of experience with communicating and with getting results, no matter how you may feel about them. You can improve your results with the same methods and tools you already know. Just pay attention to them and use them by design rather than by accident.

By thinking of results as a function of communicating, you can intentionally influence the results you get. You can do this by a process which may seem fairly simple:

- Pay attention to the form as well as the content of the messages you send and receive.
- Judge how well you are doing by the responses your messages receive.
- Adjust the messages you send according to the result you want, your situation, and the responses your messages get.

That may be easier said than done, so the rest of the book deals with how to do it.

How We Communicate

"Actions speak louder than words." "It's not what you say, it's how you say it." "Your lips tell me no-no, but there's yes-yes in your eyes." "Increase your word power." "Read between the lines." These are a few examples of how we communicate. *Everything we do sends some kind of message.*

Our society puts so much emphasis on words and other symbols that we tend to disregard the other aspects of communicating. If we concentrate on words, however, we may miss the real message. Edward T. Hall wrote, "Human beings live in a single world of communication, but they divide that world into two parts: words and behavior (verbal and nonverbal)."

Words

Words, like money, are easy-to-handle symbols which represent something else. Without money farmers would take a load of grain or hogs to the store; steel workers would get paid in ingots; and government workers in red tape.

Without words we would have no dictionaries, crossword puzzles or computer manuals. We could not discuss religion, politics or legal technicalities.

Although the English language has more than 600,000 words, a person can communicate effectively with about 2000. The 50 most commonly used words make up 60 percent of what is spoken and 45 percent of what is written by an average person. The 500 most commonly used English words have 14,000 dictionary definitions. Here's a small sample.

> They *fly* on Random Air Lines.
> He hit a *fly* to right field.
> Time *flies* like the wind.
> Fruit *flies* like bananas.
> "Waiter, there's a *fly* in my soup."
> "That's possible. Our chef used to be a tailor."

Words mean different things in different situations. The meaning of any word depends on who's using it, the circumstances, and the words and other signals surrounding it. In certain situations people can transmit their meanings clearly even with the "wrong" words. They can also thoroughly confuse others while using the "right" words.

Three elderly Londoners were riding on a bus. The bus stopped, and one man said, "Is this Wembley?" Another said, "No, this is Thursday," and the third said, "So am I. Let's get off and have a drink."

Like those Londoners, we respond to words, and to other kinds of messages, according to our own experiences and according to what we *think* we heard or saw. These responses do not necessarily have any relation to the senders' intentions.

Like fire, words have made great contributions to civilization, and when we use them, we must be careful.

Behavior

Communicating without words is a familiar idea. "You look happy." "Smile when you say that." "You don't sound sincere." Few people realize, however, that *most* of the communicating process is carried on by behavior—nonverbal elements such as

- Appearance and Dress
- Body
- Facial Expression
- Voice Expression
- Movements
- Eyes
- Touching

Although we send and receive a great number and variety of messages, we ignore many of them when we don't realize they are messages. When we can overlook the obvious, it is easy to ignore the unknown.

Nonverbal signals often express a person's attitudes more accurately than words. They are less likely to be consciously controlled. By noticing nonverbal messages, we can often get even more useful information much faster than we can from words.

Before learning to read, we all communicated without words, and did it pretty well. Most of us put that process on automatic pilot and quit paying attention to it as we began to rely on words to carry our messages. In many cases, however, our automatic pilots were programmed inaccurately, so we tend to miss, or misinterpret, certain key information.

Hitting Bull's Eyes

In routine matters, such as dressing, eating, driving, and dealing with people, most of us get by pretty well. When we see and hear words and sentences, we respond to what we think they mean, and we usually get acceptable results. We see and hear a great many nonverbal messages, usually without noticing them, and we often respond to those messages in useful ways. But now we are concerned with the other times.

With the information in this book you can become a Highly Knowledgeable Communicator. You might as well do something with that knowledge. You have the tools, and you constantly communicate. By noticing the messages you send and the responses they get, you can take charge, improve your aim and get more of the responses you want. Then you get more results you want. To hit bull's eyes you need to know

- What you want (your TARGET).
- What responses/signals indicate you are ON TARGET.
- What signals you get related to your TARGET.
- What kinds of messages get the responses you want.

A journey of a thousand miles begins with a single step. And so does any other journey. Whether the results you want are simple or complex, the journey to intentionally achieving them begins with the step of setting up a TARGET.

PART 2
TARGET ON RESULTS

OFFICIAL 100 YARD SMALL BORE TARGET

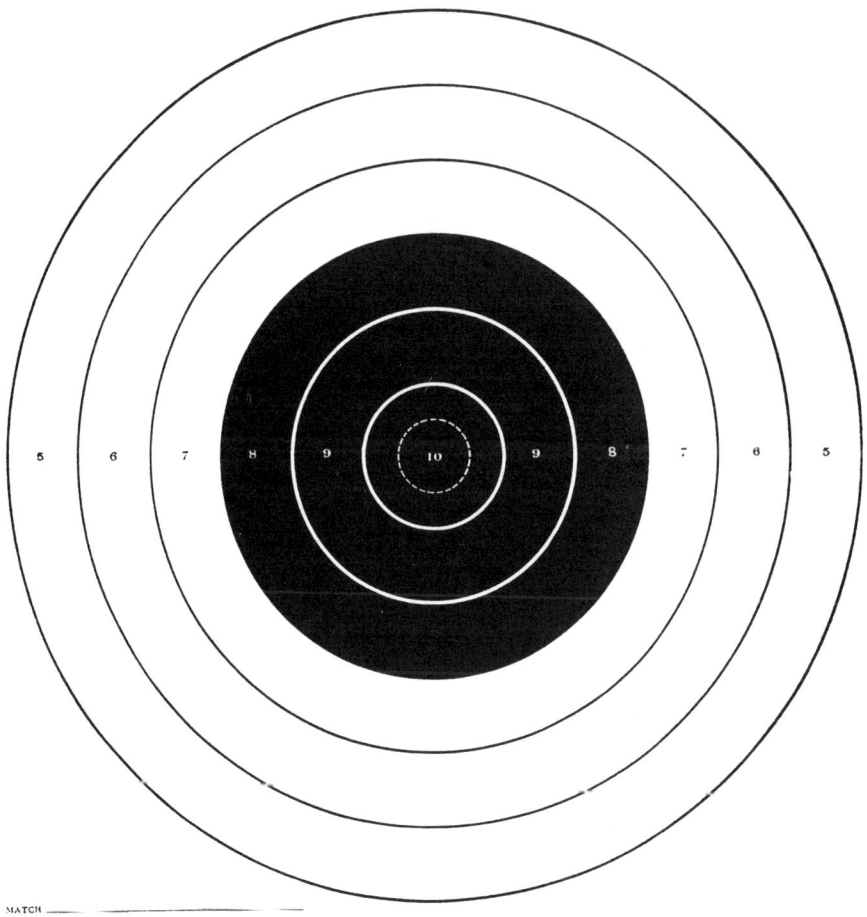

> I had a target in mind.
> *Lee Iacocca*

TARGET ON RESULTS

Many people claim to be experts, but few can produce an expert badge. I can, and here is a picture of it. What, you may ask, does this Expert Rifleman badge have to do with the subject under discussion? There is a connection. They both have to do with hitting targets. I received the badge when I was in the Army, but I started to earn it several years before.

When I was about six my dad gave me a cut-down single-shot .22 rifle and basic instruction. Then, when he was there to supervise, I shot at targets like the one on the previous page. We had a good time and hit lots of targets with this approach:

Safety	Treat every firearm as if it is loaded. Keep it unloaded with the safety on, except when actually shooting at a target. NEVER point a gun, real or toy, at anyone.
Target	Set up targets that are easy to see and within range.
Zero	Brace the rifle to keep it steady, fire three shots at a target, check where they hit, and adjust the sights.
Aim	In shooting position, line the sights on the bull's eye.
Breathe	Take a deep breath and hold it.
Shoot	Squeeze (don't pull or jerk) the trigger *only* when the sights are properly aligned.
Check	Find out where the shot hit.
Adjust	If the shot is not in the bull's eye, readjust the sights or do whatever else it takes to get on target.
Practice	Do all this until you consistently hit bull's eyes.

That is a brief summary of the process which can put you on the Olympic Rifle Team, if you stay with it. But I bring it up for another reason. This process also works for pistol shooting, and archery. In modified form it applies to basketball, baseball, football, darts, tennis, and golf. You can also use those steps, figuratively, for hitting TARGETS in all areas of life.

First take these practical steps to set up easy-to-hit TARGETS.

T - THINK OF A RESULT YOU WANT

This essential, but often overlooked. You can't hit a TARGET if you don't have one. Thinking of a result alerts your mind, and you begin to notice and think of things which lead to that result.

If you don't know what you want, think what your result will do for you, and go from there.

A - AIM FOR A POSITIVE RESULT

Think of the result you want as a positive accomplishment so you have something specific to aim for. If you're thinking of something you don't want, figure out what you'd rather have.

R - REFINE THE DETAILS

Think of your result in detail. Ask questions if necessary. What? Who? Where? When? What will you see when you have that result? What will you hear? What will you feel?

G - GET INTO IT

When you clearly see, hear, and feel what your TARGET will be like, mentally step into the scene. Experience that result as realistically as you can. Make adjustments if necessary. Notice how you feel. Now decide if you *really* want that result.

E - EXPAND YOUR TEAM

If other people are involved with this TARGET, identify them, qualify them, find out what they want, and figure out how getting that they want will also get what you want. If it can be done, at a fair price, get on their side to hit their TARGET.

T - TURN TO KEY CLUES

Identify the key nonverbal clues which tell you you're ON TARGET or off base. Keep those signs in mind to steer by.

> Target On Results For Results On Target

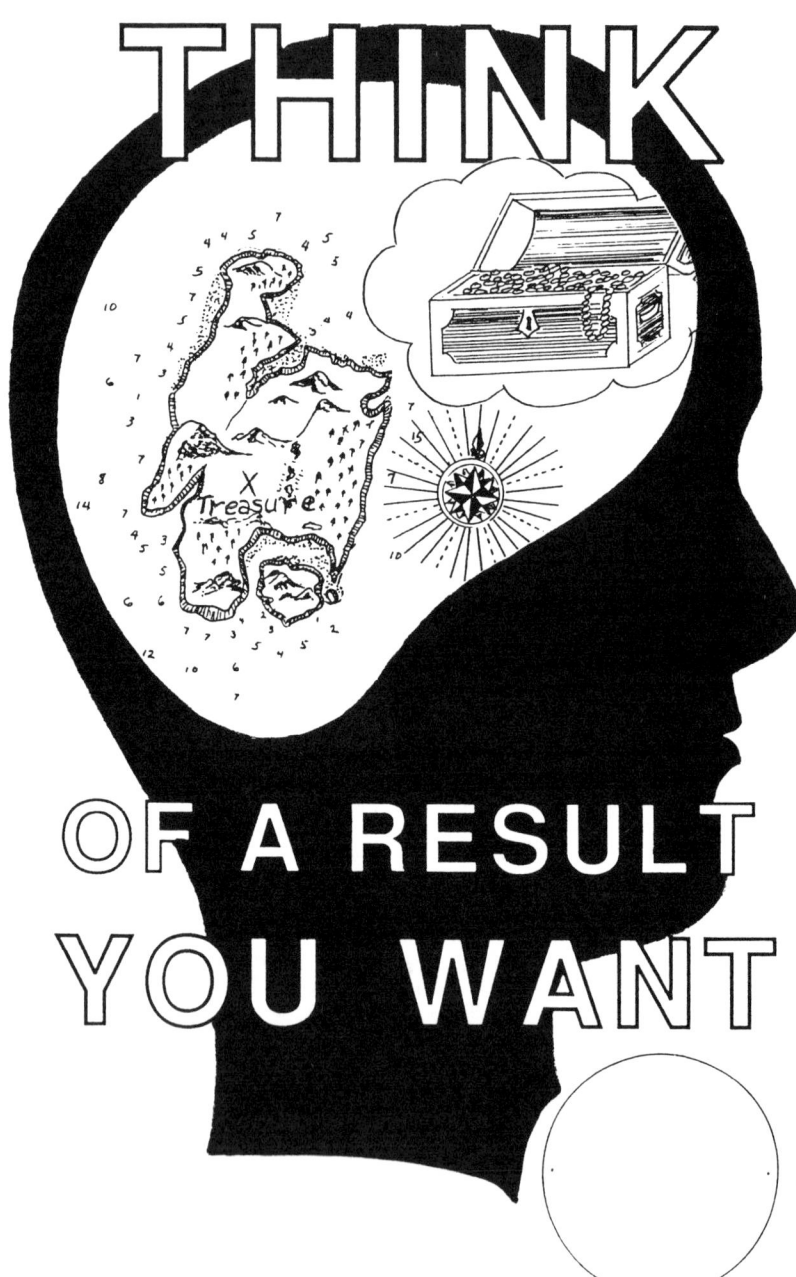

> We know that the ancestor of
> every action is a thought.
> *Ralph Waldo Emerson*

> I think I can. I think I can.
> *The Little Engine That Could*

3
THINK OF A RESULT YOU WANT

Pieces of eight! Gold doubloons! Precious jewels!

Hunting treasure across the ocean was the farthest thing from the mind of young Jim Hawkins and his friends, Dr. Livesy and Squire Trelawney—until they saw the old pirate's map. They did not notice such things as ships, sailing, supplies, crews, currents, navigation, winds, tides, treasures and pirates. But when they began to think about the treasure, they were soon aware of those things and more.

Robert Louis Stevenson's *Treasure Island* is the story of Jim, an innkeeper's son, and his adventures, which began when an old sea captain came to stay at the inn. The captain paid Jim to "keep a weather-eye out for a seafaring man with one leg." No one-legged man showed up, but Jim saw some mean-looking, rough-talking men quarrel with the captain. Shortly after that the captain died, and in his sea chest Jim found a map of an island with an X marking the location of the treasure of the notorious pirate, Captain Flint.

Jim took the map to Dr. Livesy and Squire Trelawney, and they began to think about ways to recover the treasure. In those days the only way to get to an island was by sea, so the two men and the lad, none of whom knew much about the sea, were soon thinking of ways to outfit a ship to sail across the ocean. They knew they wanted to get to the spot marked by the X, and they began to notice things related to getting there, things they had previously ignored.

Soon after they first thought of the treasure, Squire Trelawney had gone to the nearest seaport, bought a ship, hired a crew, and the three were happily sailing to Treasure Island.

Thinking of a TARGET *is like marking it on a map.* Once you set your sights on it, you begin to explore ways to get to that spot. You notice information from outside sources, and solutions "just come to you" from someplace in the back of your mind.

"Think of a result you want" may seem obvious, but one of my jobs is to keep you from overlooking the obvious. The useful obvious, that is. Most people going the Random way do so because they overlooked this obvious step. Jim and the doctor and the squire would never get to Treasure Island on Random Ship Lines, because no ship lines went near that island.

If you don't think about a result you want, how will you know when you get it? There is more to thinking about it than meets the eye or ear—both in the processes involved and in the benefits gained.

Thinking of a result you want sets up a chain of events leading to that result. The moment you think of it, your result becomes a TARGET, and some remarkable mental processes begin to zero in on it. You may notice some of this activity, but most of it goes on behind the scenes. You may forget about a TARGET until you notice a piece of valuable information, you become aware of possibilities you never knew about before, or you suddenly realize a problem is solved.

Sometimes thinking about a TARGET is the only step you need. You are likely to get what you think about, so be careful. Think about things you *really* want.

On the other hand, thinking of TARGETS for other people is a waste of time and it can lead to frustration, so I suggest you concentrate on TARGETS which are under your control. Of course you will often have other people involved in your own TARGETS, and we will deal with them in Chapters 7 and 8.

How We Think

Few of us notice *how* we think, so bringing these elements to your attention gives you a chance to use them to your advantage.

We think by using our senses. Our thoughts are made up of various combinations of seeing, hearing and feeling information—sometimes smelling and tasting.

Most people are aware that we use our five senses when we receive information from the outside. Few people realize that we use those senses to process that information—when we "picture things in our mind" or "hear a tune in our heads" or "remember the feeling of a cool spray of water on a hot day."

Think of some ways we describe thinking processes: "I had a brilliant flash!" "It just hit me." "It rang a bell." We are so used to expressions like those that most of us don't think about them, nor about the idea that thinking of an event triggers physical responses similar to those brought on by the actual event. Recalling a particular conversation, for instance, reactivates the same seeing, hearing, and feeling channels which processed the original experience, so that experience and the memory of it must be similar. They vary, of course. Some memories are "dim," "faint," or "hazy." Others are "clear," "distinct," or "vivid." Some are even distorted when these channels mix in unrelated information.

Two Ways of Thinking

Let's use *verbal* and *nonverbal* to describe two ways of thinking.

Verbal Thinking	*Nonverbal Thinking*	
Words and other symbols	Pictures	Smells
	Feelings	Tastes
	Sounds	

Most of us are capable of both verbal and nonverbal thinking, although many of us get into a habit of using one or the other. Each has advantages. Nonverbal thinking has the advantage of being closer to an actual experience.

If Frank Flowers picks a rose, he will see the colors, size, shape and texture of its petals, leaves, stem and thorns. He will smell its fragrance. He may feel its texture, size, temperature and shape. If he gets a thorn in his thumb, he will *really* feel it. Then he might hear his own voice yelling, "Ouch!" That is how Frank takes in information about that rose. That is his experience with that flower.

He can tell it is a rose, what kind of rose, and much more by comparing what he sees with information he has stored from past experiences with roses. If he names the things he sees, hears, feels and smells, and if he describes that experience in words, then he is thinking verbally. If he wants to order a rose bush from the nursery, he must think verbally to fill out an order and add up the charges.

If Frank wants to look especially spiffy, he can think of that TARGET by forming a mental picture of himself with a rosebud in his lapel. Or he can say to himself, "I want a rosebud for my lapel." Then he looks in his garden for a bud about that size. Sound will not help him much with roses.

Marilyn Medley, however, selects music to play on a radio station. Sight won't help Marilyn a great deal. Compact discs look pretty much alike, and they feel about the same. Records and tapes present the same situation. Marilyn has to judge them by the sounds they produce. She listens to the music, compares it with her accumulated information on music, and decides whether the selection is a hit or a miss.

Every experience we have gives us information for all five senses, though all of it may not register with us consciously. Taste, for example, is insignificant in most experiences outside the kitchen and dining room. We tend to notice odors only when they are unusual or strong.

Of the other three forms of information—seeing, hearing and feeling—we tend to pick favorites in certain situations. Sometimes it is necessary—Frank Floral would miss his TARGET by listening for a rosebud, and feeling for it could be painful.

We usually have choices, however. What do you notice most about a car, a house, an office, a person? The sounds? Full-dimension stereo, crackling fire, melodious voice? The feelings? Five-way adjustable seat and smooth ride, warm cozy atmosphere, dead-fish handshake? Or the sights? Sleek black exterior, shiny modern furnishings, stylishly dressed?

At this point in the process it is important that you think of something you want, even if it is vague. You will have opportunities to adjust and refine later. The only thing that can slow you down is not knowing what you want.

'BUT I DON'T KNOW WHAT I WANT!'

Utility companies are bound to make huge profits from the electricity used by people holding refrigerator doors open as they wonder what they want to eat. When you don't know what you want, looking in the refrigerator may help. And it may complicate matters if you find several tempting morsels. That's all right. Life is full of choices. Here are some ways to

find out what you want from your refrigerator or from any other situation.
- Think of what it will do for you.
- Select from a menu.
- Go from what you don't want.

Let's Get to the Bottom of This: What Will It Do For You?

Monica Motrine—obviously a soap-opera character—wants money. Specifically, she wants $2,500,000. Monica really knows what she wants, doesn't she? Not exactly. She knows what she thinks she wants. But money, like many other announced objectives, is not an end in itself. It is only a means to an end.

What does Monica want the money for? What will it do for her? Will it rescue her lover, Raoul Montegrey, from a hostile takeover? Will it pay for her mother's operation? Will it allow her to ruin the people who kept her off the high school basketball team? Will it let her finish her research on a formula that will make the world a healthier, happier place to live in?

We don't know about Monica, but you know about you. What will that result do for you? You might ask yourself the question, several times, to get to the heart of the matter. You may realize your first answers, like *Money*, might be routes to a TARGET rather than the TARGET itself.

We could ask Monica, "What would $2,500,000 do for you?"
"Allow me to take over Acme Amalgamated Corp."
"What will that do for you?"
"Let me to ruin Peggy Pert, Paul Pepper and their families."
"And what will that do for you?"
"Avenge me for not making the school basketball team."
"And what will that do for you?"
"Help me regain my self respect."
"What will that do for you?"
"Let me hold my head up and feel good about myself."

So by asking that question a few times we strip away the layers and get to what she really wants. Ask that question about any result you want. Reducing a TARGET to this basic level can save you a lot of effort and give you more satisfying results.

Monica might actually get her $2,500,000 and buy a controlling interest in Acme Amalgamated only to find that the equipment wore out, Brazil took over the market, and Peggy and Paul moved to Memphis. All her time and effort is wasted, she is worse off than before, and she missed out on many easier, and more pleasant, ways to hold her head up and feel good about herself.

If you continue to ask what each result you mention will do for you, eventually you can go no farther, and you will probably arrive at some kind of feeling you would like to have. In his book on winning and keeping customers, Michael LeBoef says we only "buy" two things, good feelings and solutions to problems—and solving a problem usually results in good feelings.

So what gives you the feeling you want? Answering that question might give you a menu—a choice of several things which give you the feeling you want. Pick the one which looks, sounds, or feels best to be your TARGET.

Select From A Menu

Menus work well for restaurants and computer programs. They tell people what is available and let them choose what they want. You can do the same thing to select your TARGETS, although you may have to make up the menu yourself.

You may find menus in the form of lists, catalogs, or other publications. To make your own menu you can either tap your own stores of knowledge to list the possibilities, or you can investigate wherever seems appropriate to get the information. Just make sure that the list is as complete as possible, then pick out the items which are most attractive to you. As you follow through the process, you will have opportunities to revise, adapt and tailor any result you select to fit your particular needs, tastes and circumstances.

What You Don't Want

Most counselors, psychotherapists and consultants I know agree that people who come to them with a problem usually do not know what they want. Once they find out, getting it seems to be no problem. Quite often, though, they do know what they don't want.

That will do—for a start. If you know what you don't want, you can turn that into something you do want. The next chapter tells how to do that.

Plant a Seed

Thinking of a result plants a little seed in the fertile field of your mind. You may not notice it for a while, but the nutrients of knowledge and experience, combined with rays of information and raindrops of resources get that seed germinating. It grows strong roots and a little shoot appears above the surface. You are still not aware of everything that goes on in the process, but you can see the shoot growing taller and stronger until at last it produces the fruits you had in mind when you planted that seed.

Think Review

Think of a Result You Want.
  Form mental images, or
  Put your thoughts into words.
Think of a result for you, not for someone else.
Think of what you want, not what someone else wants you to want.
If You Don't Know What You Want,
  Figure out what it will do for you, or
  Select from a menu.

Accentuate The Positive
Johnny Mercer

Thinking *sand trap* or *pond* is negative golf. Thinking *green* is positive, target golf.
Roy Pace

4
AIM FOR A POSITIVE RESULT

H. G. Wells wrote a story about a man who invented a miraculous brew, which he gave to an overweight man named Pyecraft. The inventor went to visit and found Mr. Pyecraft floating in a corner of the ceiling. As he described the scene,

> It was really a most extraordinary spectacle, that great, fat, apoplectic-looking man upside down and trying to get from the ceiling to the floor. "That prescription," he said. "Too successful."'
> "How?"
> "Loss of weight—almost complete."
> And then, of course, I understood.
> "By Jove, Pyecraft," said I, "what you wanted was a cure for *fatness*! But you always called it *weight*."

If you are thinking of a negative result—something you don't want—something you want to avoid, escape, lose or quit—now is the time to make your TARGET a positive accomplishment—something specific you want to do, have, or be. If Pyecraft had said, "I want to be slim," he would not have become a weightless fat man bouncing off the ceiling.

Go to a ticket agent for any existing air line and say, "I want to get out of town." You won't get far. The agent wants to know where you are going and when. Otherwise you get no ticket.

When you say, "I want to go to Kansas City Tuesday morning," the agent says, "How will you be paying for that?"

A positive result automatically avoids what you don't want, and it also keeps you from jumping out of the frying pan into the fire. Ohio State football coach Woody Hayes was quoted as saying, "Three things can happen when you throw the football, and only one of them is good." A lot of things can happen on the Random way, and, compared with the present situation, they can be worse, much worse, about the same, and maybe better. When you want something definitely better, it pays to improve your chances with a positive TARGET. It also decreases your chances of having to go through this again later.

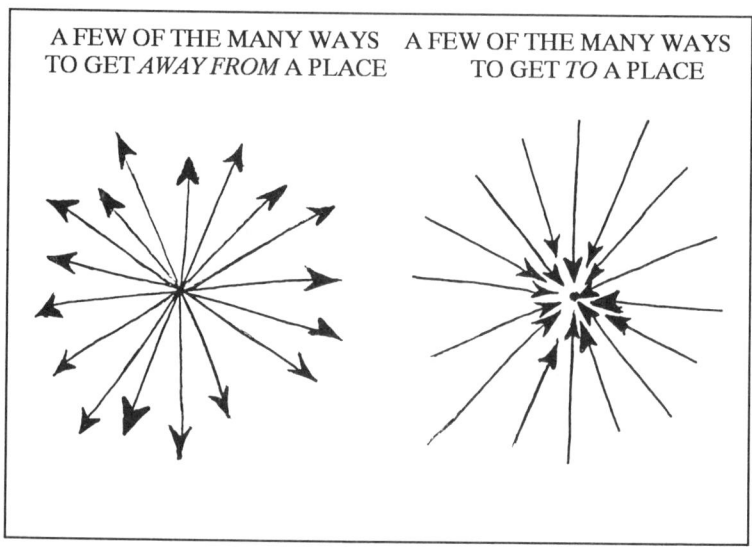

A FEW OF THE MANY WAYS TO GET *AWAY FROM* A PLACE

A FEW OF THE MANY WAYS TO GET *TO* A PLACE

The positive TARGET discussed in this chapter is not the same kind of positive as in Norman Vincent Peale's *The Power of Positive Thinking* or W. Clement Stone's *positive mental attitude*. Peale and Stone are talking about an "I can do it" approach to life's challenges. That kind of approach is valuable, and we will deal with ways of using it in Chapter 10. But a positive TARGET is one you can aim at and do something about.

Aiming for a positive result lets you avoid what you want to avoid or get away from what you want to get away from. It also gives you just one TARGET to shoot for instead of many; it gives you a specific TARGET to focus on instead of a shot in the dark; and it concentrates your efforts and your resources on that one TARGET.

Connirae and Steve Andreas have explored people's mental images a good deal, and most of the people they studied described positive TARGETS as bright and colorful, whereas the pictures of things they wanted to get away from tended to be dim and gray. So for a bright future, aim for a positive TARGET.

Here are some examples of negative and positive ways of saying the same thing.

Negative	Positive
Get out of the house	Walk to the park
Avoid losing	Win
Cut down on fat	Eat more vegetables
Not have an accident	Drive safely
Not feel bad	Feel good
Lose weight	Be slimmer
Avoid punishment	Gain rewards

Reading the negative column, I feel gray, heavy and gloomy. Fortunately, the words in the other column and the brighter images they produce cheer me up.

A Short Demonstration

For the rest of this chapter please DO NOT think of a Blue Kangaroo.

THIS IS A PICTURE OF PEOPLE NOT DOING SOMETHING. CAN YOU GUESS WHAT THEY ARE NOT DOING?

The only way we can specifically *not* think of something is to think of it. The only way we can think about *not* doing something is to think about doing it. Think about it. Think about not crossing a street.

Some people will see a mental picture of crossing the street, then freeze it, cross it out, erase it, run it backward, or somehow indicate that action is not to take place. Others will hear the words, "Do not cross the street." Some will feel themselves starting to cross a street, then feel themselves being stopped or pulled back. We have many ways to think of not crossing the street, but they all involve thinking of crossing the street.

Remember, thinking about a result stimulates your mental resources to get that result. What happens when you think about not crossing the street, not eating chocolate, not dropping the ball? The images in your mind are of crossing the street, eating chocolate and dropping the ball. *This improves your chances of getting exactly what you don't want.*

This may help explain how so many of us find ourselves doing things we resolved we would never do again.

Now what happens when you think of staying on the sidewalk, eating celery and catching the ball?

Make It Positive

Tom Hardy does not like to go to work, and he wants to do something about it. He knows what he doesn't want. But now it's time to brighten up the picture and pick a positive TARGET. Here is how he might narrow it down.

Doesn't Want	*Wants*
Present job as it is	Anything else
Present job as it is	Any job he is qualified for
Present job as it is	A job in the same industry in the same area
Present job as it is	A better job with the same company
Present job as it is	Present job with more money and more responsibility

As long as Tom thinks about what he *doesn't* want, he thinks about his present job as it is. By turning to what he *does* want, Tom focuses on things he wants in a job, and he realizes he already has a lot of them. We don't know what he means by "more money" and "more responsibility," but refining TARGETS comes in the next chapter. Tom now has a positive, though fuzzy, result in mind. If he got stuck on the negative, Tom might have quit his job and missed out on what he really wanted.

What Would You Rather Have?

Sometimes turning a negative wish into a positive TARGET involves concentrating on the key factors in depth as in Tom's case. Sometimes it can be as simple as picking more appropriate words—"stay on" rather than "not fall off," for example. In any case the key question for those who only know what they don't want is, "What would you rather have?" Answer that and you clear your way to aim for a positive result.

A few people might have a problem answering that question. They tend to think exclusively of going away from the undesirable rather than going toward the desirable. But even people who think in terms of avoiding the unpleasant can benefit by having positive TARGETS. Then they can also avoid many future unpleasant situations as well as one present one.

People who can think of going toward the pleasant—that includes most of us—can think of pleasant results they would like to have rather than the unpleasant situation they want to get away from. When they do, they have a positive TARGET.

No matter what kind of results you want, Roy Pace's thoughts from *Target Golf* will probably apply.

> Concentrating on precisely where you want to put the ball produces a positive approach to playing the game. Because there are so many obvious hazards on a golf course, it is natural to have them in the forefront of your mind as you consider a shot and prepare to play it. Playing target golf helps you exclude these distractions.

Aim Review

To have the best chance of getting what you want, make sure you think of your TARGET as a positive result.

A positive TARGET lets you concentrate your resources.

It helps you avoid what you don't want.

Turn negative wishes into positive TARGETS by determining what you would like to have instead.

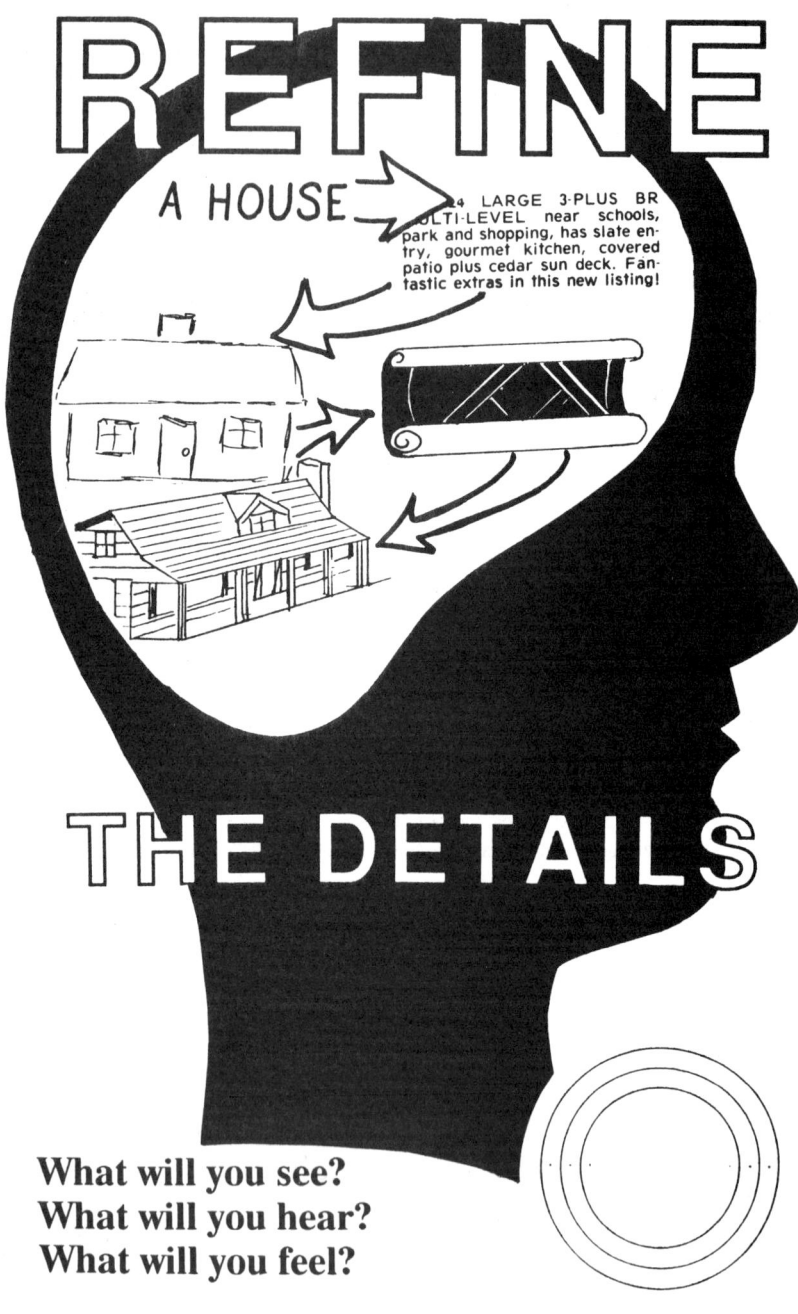

What will you see?
What will you hear?
What will you feel?

> How do you want that cooked?
> What kind of salad dressing?
> *A Waiter*

> Could you be more specific?
> *A Good Reporter*

5
REFINE THE DETAILS

Hundreds of protesting residents were evicted from a San Francisco apartment hotel so foreign investors could start construction on the site. Three years later the spot was still a hole in the ground, because the investors did not know what they were going to build.

Those investors were unusual only in the amount of publicity their problem got. Having a fuzzy idea of the results we want is quite common, but most of us don't demonstrate the fact in the middle of a large city.

Prospectors in the Old West spent years roaming deserts and mountains searching for "pay dirt." Sometimes they might find gold nuggets or dust, but most of the "strikes" were ores with a low pay-to-dirt ratio. Today one mine in Nevada produces one *ounce* of gold from two and a half *tons* of *high-grade* ore. Imagine what low-grade ore is like.

Nobody would try to make gold coins or herringbone chains from that ore until it was refined so he had metal to work with.

Sometimes our ideas are nuggets, pure and ready to use. More often our first thoughts come as ore, and we need to refine them before we have anything to get results with.

If you have been following the steps so far, you have thought of a result which is

- Something *you* want.
- Something within your control.
- A positive action toward a specific TARGET.

36 • TARGET ON RESULTS

This chapter takes you further along in the refining process so you can have a TARGET which is

- Clearly defined.
- Easy to recognize when you reach it.
- Easier to reach.

With a clearly-defined TARGET you can concentrate your resources and energy on one spot, because you know where to focus or tune in. A laser is a beam of concentrated light which can carve wood, do delicate surgery and guide missiles. But without the concentration, it's just a light. A highly-directional microphone can pick up one voice at a football game. Ordinary microphones pick up the whole crowd.

Refine

Can you imagine the following conversation between Bert Baron, the investor, and Mark Mason, the builder?

Bert: I've decided I need a new building, and I would like your company to build it.
Mark: Thank you for your confidence in Mason Construction. We'll be happy to build your building. I'll get a crew started on it real soon.
Bert: I appreciate your help.
Mark: That's what we're here for. If we can do anything else for you, just let me know.
Bert: I'll do that. Well, I guess I'll run along. Good-bye.
Mark: Good-bye. Thanks for the business.
Bert: You're welcome. See you around. (Exit)

Wasn't something missing? If these people have any sense at all, they need more details about that building, such as:

What kind of building?
What size?
What shape?
Where will it be?
When is it to be finished?
What will it look like?
How much will it cost?
How will it be paid for?

They need to know everything down to door knobs and light switches. Builders work from blueprints which show every detail of the structure so it will turn out right the first time.

By refining the details, you put on your architect hat and turn vague ideas into blueprints that make sense.

Ask

> Child: Daddy, how does the television work?
> Father: I don't know.
> Child: Daddy, where does electricity come from?
> Father: I don't know.
> Child: Daddy, what makes the grass grow?
> Father: I don't know.
> Child: Daddy, do you mind if I ask you all these questions?
> Father: Of course not. You can't learn anything if you don't ask questions.

We live in the Information Age with a lot of emphasis on having the right answers. Asking the right questions seems to get overlooked, but not here. In this case the questions most likely to get answers which refine your original thought into a sharp, clear TARGET are:

- What?
- Who
- How
- Where?
- When?
- What will you see when you have your result?
- What will you hear?
- What will you feel?

Answering these questions in terms of what you will actually see (people, places, furnishings, signs, papers, colors, shapes), hear (voices, words, music, machinery, volume, tone, rhythm), and feel (furniture, equipment, clothing, temperature, texture, pressure) as realistically as possible helps you set up a specific, detailed, refined TARGET, the easiest kind to hit. You may not need to use all these questions. If you started out with a clear idea of what your TARGET looks, sounds and feels like, you may not need any of them.

Bert Baron, of course, needs all of them. Here is one way to deal with his vague idea about a building.

> Q: What building?
> A: A luxury hotel.

Q: What do you mean by luxury?
A: State-of-the-art features, elegant decor, gourmet restaurants, high prices and a waterfall in the lobby.
Q: What features? What do you mean by state-of-the-art? What decor? What do you mean by elegant? How many restaurants? What kind of cuisine? What prices? What is high? What kind of waterfall?

These *What?* questions will take a lot of time as we get down to details, so let's move on to some of the other questions.

Q: How will you build it?
A: Form a limited partnership to raise money, hire an architect to draw up the plans, take an option on the land and hire a contractor.
Q: How will you form a limited partnership? How much money will you raise? How will you take an option? Where is the land? Who will be the limited partners? Which architect? What contractor? When will this happen?

Well, one thing leads to another when you start asking questions, and some projects involve more detail than others. By the time Bert gets down to the light switches and shower curtains and all the other details, he will have gone through a lot of *What, Who, How, When* and *Where* questions.

See, Hear, Feel

The purpose of asking those questions is to get you to think of the result you want in as much detail as possible. In fact, the idea is for you to compose a realistic mental image of your TARGET—to see, hear and feel exactly what that experience will be like.

When your TARGET involves things you have done, had or been before, you can remember what you saw, heard and felt during the past experiences. When your TARGET is something you will do, have, or be for the first time, you can compose a scenario based on information you have gathered from your own experiences, others' experiences, and your own creativity.

When you have those images in mind, your mental resources have a TARGET to aim for. In the next chapter you'll find a way to use those images to find out if that TARGET is what you *really* want. You should know that before you go any farther.

Refine Review

Refine your fuzzy or abstract ideas to specific details; make a blueprint for your TARGET.
Eliminate the non-essential material with questions
    What?   What will you see?
    Who?   What will you hear?
    How?   What will you feel?
    Where?
    When?
    When you know exactly what you will see, hear and feel, when you hit your TARGET, you are ready to put that information into action.

> Beware your desires, for surely
> you shall attain them.
> *Old Saying*

> I practice juggling in my mind.
> Oops!
> *Steve Martin*

6

GET INTO IT

When Lou Brock was setting major league records for stealing bases, he would rehearse several times before he left first base. In his mind he ran through every detail. He saw the pitcher, the infielders, the dirt, the grass, the base, the catcher's throw. He heard his footsteps on the base path, the smack of the ball in the infielder's glove. He felt his legs and arms moving, the dirt and the slide into second base, the infielder's tag—too late. After stealing the base four or five times in his mind, Brock stole it again for the record.

Jack Nicklaus has been quoted many times as saying he pictures each shot in his mind before he makes it on a golf course.

This process has many uses. Sales people, for example, mentally plan, rehearse, and polish their presentations and the ways they handle objections before they make sales calls.

With mental rehearsal we can develop skills and confidence. For example, *Sports Illustrated* reported:

> An Australian study shows that basketball players who mentally rehearsed free throws shooting improved their accuracy by an average of 23% over those who didn't.

This practice is also known as *visualization*, but notice that Brock rehearsed the sounds and feelings as well as the visual aspects of stealing a base. Robert McKim covers all the bases in his book, *Experiences in Visual Thinking*.

> Now imagine that in your hand you have a delicious, crisp apple. Feel the apple's coolness; its weight; its firmness; its round volume; its waxy smoothness.... Now bite the apple; hear its juicy snap; savor its texture, its flavor. Smell the apple's sweet fragrance.

There is more to an apple than meets the eye. To fully appreciate an apple, even an imaginary one, we must use all of our senses.

Like many things we do without realizing it, mental rehearsal or visualization can have its drawbacks. Many people think so much about what could go wrong that they are rehearsing to fail. And this process works. They succeed—at failing. You can avoid that sort of thing by selecting positive TARGETS. So ~~don't forget~~ remember to rehearse only what you want to happen.

Testing TARGETS

Yes, you can improve skills and confidence, solve problems, design and invent things in your mind. And you can use the same mental process to test a result you *think* you want to make sure it is a TARGET you *really* want.

When we order clothing by mail, we think we know what we will get. From a catalog's picture and description we have an idea of what the clothing looks and feels like, but we don't know for sure until we actually see it and try it on.

In a store we can see and feel the clothes. We can try them on and find out how they fit. If necessary, we can have them altered so they fit perfectly.

Electronics firms in California often hire talented people from the East Coast at great expense. Recruiting, moving, training, salaries and other expenses can easily add up to more than $100,000 per person. Yet new people are often gone within six months. Obviously some people didn't like what they got.

Have you ever heard, or said, "I don't know why I ever wanted that"? Wanting something, getting it, then realizing we don't like it is a common experience. A situation may look or sound good, but you don't know for sure until you experience it.

When you order a shirt which turns out to be unsatisfactory, the consequences aren't usually serious. Mail order houses have regular procedures for returning merchandise. Taking a job in another part of the country, buying a house, starting a business, and other major transactions can have serious consequences. They seldom have exchange or refund policies.

If you had a way you could try on other results the way you do clothing, you could find out in advance how you will feel about them. This would save you a lot of time, effort, and problems pursuing TARGETS you won't like when you get them. Well, you can do just that in the video/sound/feel production studio of your mind. There you have facilities for designing and producing realistic mental experiences. You can set up a scenario, test it, and correct anything you don't like. In split seconds, at no cost or risk, you can have a custom-designed TARGET.

Of course you can't think of everything that could possibly happen, but you can get a feeling of the situation. If you don't have enough information to produce a realistic mental experience, you probably need more details.

You are likely to get results you think about, so doesn't t make sense to make sure you want to live with those results?

The Studio of Your Mind

Most people can see, hear, and feel experiences in their minds—whether they remember the experiences or create them. For example, it is easy to think of what your day will be like a week from tomorrow, even though you must think of something that has not yet happened. Thinking of the future is usually based on past experience, of course, and probabilities.

A few people, however, are like the woman who said, "I can't see pictures in my head. Is there anything I can do?" I asked her to describe a scene from the last movie she saw. She described the scene, the actors, the theater, and the seats. She could not have done that in such detail without "seeing" that scene in her head. She did do it without being aware of seeing anything. This can happen, and there are ways to become more aware of what you see, hear, and feel mentally and to produce realistic experiences in the studio of your mind.

- Bill Russell would watch a player on the basketball court, then close his eyes and make an instant replay on the inside of his eyelids. The more he did it, the more complete the pictures became.
- Bandler and Grinder recommend going from a sense you are aware of to one you don't notice. For example, if you can hear the ocean in your head, listen to it for a while, then begin to feel the water, the sand, the sun, and the wind. Then think what it looks like, and soon you'll see it.
- When people process visual information, they usually look up or stare straight ahead, breathe high in the chest, talk

high and fast, and use seeing words. If you want to see mental pictures, get in a seeing attitude: Look up, talk high and fast, breathe high in the chest, and use seeing words. Refer to the chart on page 124 for ways to get access to seeing, hearing, and feeling information.

If you sit comfortably in a chair, relax, and breathe deeply a few times, you can see, hear, and feel enough to set the scene for your TARGET. You wouldn't want it if you couldn't imagine it. Then just fill in the details.

Get into the Scene

The purpose of Chapter 5 was to refine your TARGET to the details you will see, hear and feel when you hit it. This chapter takes you a step farther as you mentally experience that result and evaluate your responses to it.

1. Think of having the result you want.
   a. See exactly what is there to the smallest detail;
   b. Hear the sounds that go with it;
   c. Feel the temperature, textures, pressure, etc.;
   d. Smell any odors you associate with that TARGET;
   e. Taste whatever tastes might be appropriate.

In other words get into that situation with all your senses as much as you can. And be sure to include any responses you will see, hear and feel from other people involved which indicate to you that you have succeeded.

2. While you are in this experience, notice your emotional responses, the feelings inside that let you know whether this situation is comfortable, painful, just right, needs alterations, etc.

3. Be alert for words of warning, feelings of foreboding or pictures of unhappy consequences. Pay attention to these signs of dissatisfaction. They can become self-fulfilling prophecies.

4. If you have any unfavorable reactions to your experience, identify the things you were reacting to.

5. Go back to step one, replay the scene, and alter those parts which triggered unfavorable reactions. Now go through it again and notice your responses.

6. Continue to alter and adjust until either you go through the entire experience feeling the way you want to, or you decide you do not want this result after all.

It is easier to adjust a pattern than to alter a completed suit, and it is easier to abandon a project in the planning stage than during construction or after it is finished. This is a splendid time to make sure you want this TARGET, that you can live with the TARGET once you have it. If it does not feel right, do what it takes to make it comfortable.

Getting into the experience does several things for you.

- It solidifies your experience of succeeding, and it establishes a pattern in your mind—marks it on the map, so to speak. And you have already done it at least once.
- It makes you aware of what the experience looks, sounds and feels like, so you will recognize it when it happens.
- It puts the experience pattern on record so it becomes a TARGET for your mental tracking devices.
- It gives you the opportunity to alter that experience and make it comfortable and acceptable.
- It gives you information to use in deciding whether or not to go ahead with this TARGET.

Having done all that, you are well on your way to that TARGET. Now is a good time to project it into the future. As Robert McKim says,

> Living with unforeseen consequences such as smog and traffic congestion, we are coerced into awareness of a need for foresight about the possible effects of present plans...One can rarely foresee the actual future consequences of present plans, of course. Most plans are realized in a context that contains many variables and even surprises over which the foreseer has little or no control. One can foresee alternative futures, however, a bracketed set of possibilities within which the future will likely occur.

In stories about people who are granted three wishes, the first two wishes usually produce undesirable consequences, so the people end up using the third wish to undo the first two.

You should also consider these questions.

- Where does this TARGET fit on your priority list? Will you spend too much time and energy on a low-priority result?
- Does it fit in with your long term TARGET? Will it take you away from important long range goals?

When your mental production looks, sounds and feels the way you want it, it becomes your TARGET. And if you are the only person involved in that TARGET, this is your final TARGET step. But when reaching that TARGET requires other people's cooperation or assistance, you have two more steps to take.

In Charles Dickens' *A Christmas Carol* Ebenezer Scrooge took a mental trip, saw and heard what his future would be like, and didn't feel good about it. Scrooge gathered additional information, then created a mental scene in which he felt good. Within hours of getting into that scene, Ebenezer Scrooge had the results he wanted.

Get Into It Review

Mentally experience the result you want.
See exactly what you will see.
Hear the sounds that go with it.
Feel what you will feel.
Smell and taste whatever might be appropriate.
Notice your emotional responses.
Be alert for signals of dissatisfaction of feelings of discomfort.
Replay the scene and alter whatever you need to.
Continue to alter and adjust until the result is just the way you want it, or you decide to go for something else.
Anticipate as many consequences as you can.
Keep your TARGETS consistent with long-term and higher-priority TARGETS.
Be careful what you ask for, you are likely to get it. Take time to test your TARGETS in advance.

> You can get everything in life you want if you will just help enough other people get what they want.
> *Zig Ziglar*
>
> You scratch my back, and I'll scratch yours.
> *Old Saying*

7

EXPAND YOUR TEAM

Henry Ford did not invent the automobile. Nor did he invent the assembly line. Where Ford was truly innovative, according to Lee Iacocca, "was in coming up with the $5.00 day in 1914. Five bucks was more than double what workers had been making...Henry Ford never hid his real reason for the $5.00 day: he wanted his workers to earn enough so that they could eventually buy their own cars."

To reach most TARGETS we come up with, we must deal in some way with at least one other person. When other people are involved, it is to our advantage to have them on our side and actively supporting our projects. This chapter gives you ways to

- Find out who the key people are—the ones who can make decisions and take actions that let you hit your TARGET.
- Find out what those people's TARGETS are.
- Develop a plan to hit their TARGETS and yours at the same time.
- Decide whether carrying out that plan is worth the time, energy, money, or whatever it may cost.
- Join the side of the key people and use your plan to hit their TARGETS.

Ford said, "If there is any one secret of success, it lies in the ability to get the other person's point of view and see things from his angle as well as from your own."

After selecting a TARGET from your angle, it's time to heed Henry's words—to meet the other people involved in your project and explore their points of view. If you can hit that TARGET

EXPAND YOUR TEAM

What's in it for them?

Is it worth the effort?

Hit Both Targets with One Shot

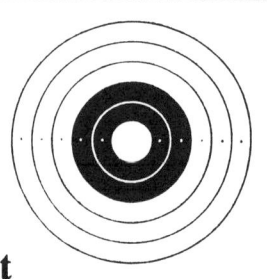

all by yourself, you won't need this step or the next one. However, if anyone besides you can influence the result you want, these steps can make your path much smoother.

Whether your TARGET is money (or what it can buy) or a partner for tennis, you will find it easier to succeed when you put human nature to work for you, neutralize any opposition, and get the key people on your side. One way to do this is to establish your position and conduct a recruiting campaign with posters, speeches and other persuasion techniques to induce those key people to come over and join you.

An easier way is to find out where they are and join them.

Once you are on their side, you are on the same side, all aiming in the same direction at a TARGET of mutual benefit and interest. Their TARGET becomes your TARGET. You become a team, combining resources to hit that TARGET.

What's in it for you? An important by-product of this joint effort is that *your* TARGET also becomes *their* TARGET, and when the team hits one TARGET, it hits both. Everybody wins.

When you follow this procedure you enhance your chances of getting your results and of avoiding unpleasant consequences. Personal relationships and businesses which thrive over the years are based on some kind of mutual benefits.

When you join "their" team,

- It becomes your team.
- The key people want to help you.
- They carry out their agreements.
- You save time and effort.
- You avoid repercussions like returns, refunds, lawsuits, and verbal or physical violence.
- You are more likely to hit your TARGET.
- Everybody can win.
- Nobody has to lose.

Let's back up a bit, though. Before we join other people's teams, we should know they are the right people.

IDENTIFY AND QUALIFY KEY PEOPLE

One day I answered the phone and heard a woman say, "I'm calling to remind Mr. Johnson of his appointment with Dr. Bennett." That woman certainly got her message across clearly, but she did not accomplish her purpose—not with that call, anyway. I had no idea who Mr. Johnson is.

It seems reasonable to send our messages to people who can affect OUR TARGET, but sometimes we spin our wheels with people who can't. Certainly if Sam Evening wants to marry Janet Summer, he will propose to her, not somebody else. But what about Bob Sellers, who wants to sell Consolidated Can Openers to Monolithic Distributors. Bob finds Paula Pursley in the manager's office and uses all his silver-tongued presentation skills convincing her that his can openers are the finest. Everything goes smoothly until Bob asks for the order and Paula says, "Well, I'm convinced, but I'll have to talk it over with my partner. He makes all those decisions."

This is known as the Absent Partner Routine. It is not a comedy act. In fact, people like Bob who get caught in it are often sad, angry, or both.

Kids get this a lot with "Ask your father," or "Ask your mother." Kids can't do much about it, but you can be prepared for the Absent Partner Routine and save your efforts for the people who can help you get your results.

Narrow The Field

Even though we have profound thoughts to express, no communicator can reasonably expect everyone to respond favorably to an identical message. We need to narrow the field. You wouldn't go from door to door proposing marriage or selling turbine generators, for instance. In most cases, when setting your sights on a TARGET, you automatically limit those involved to a few key people—often just one.

When you mentally see, hear and feel what reaching your TARGET will be like, notice the other people in the scene? Who would logically be involved in the process of getting that result? If you are legally driving a car, someone with authority to do so agreed to sell or lease it to you at a certain price—or agreed to some other arrangement. If you want a raise, you need to deal with a person who can authorize raises.

You might need some kind of response from

People with certain qualifications:	people who want new cars and can afford to pay $700 a month, people who can write a check for $20,000, people who collect postage stamps, people who like Chinese food, etc.
A type of person:	a notary public, a car dealer, a roofer, a priest, etc.
A specific person:	Dad, Mom, your boss, the municipal cout judge, etc.

Qualify

The woman who called me to remind Mr. Johnson of his appointment wasted a few minutes by dialing a wrong number. American officials trying to get hostages from the American Embassy out of Iran took ten months to find out the Iranians they were talking with had no authority in the matter.

Lee Iacocca told sales people to ask questions to "qualify" a prospect. "You've got to learn what he wants to use the car for and who else in his family will be driving it. You've also got to figure out how much he can afford."

Qualifying the people who can help you reach your TARGET saves time for everyone. It can also build good will which might pay off later. You don't have to be a salesperson to qualify people you communicate with. It is a useful process whenever you want to use your time effectively and efficiently. To qualify people, find out if they

- Can decide on the matter and act on it,
- Can use what you have to offer,
- Can do what you want them to, and
- Will do what they agree to.

When you deal only with those who qualify on all four points, you can put your efforts to more productive use. In many cases you already know whether people qualify or not. Sometimes you can find out before serious communicating starts, and sometimes you have to find out on the spot.

Can They Decide and Act?

In situations involving people you know, this question may not be necessary, but if you haven't thought about it, you could be surprised. If you have even a shadow of a doubt, find out. When you want a response from a corporation, a government agency, even a married couple, you will do well to find out in advance. Otherwise you may end up in the "Absent Partner" routine.

For *partner* you can substitute husband, wife, consultant, accountant, lawyer, home office, bureau chief, etc. Sometimes people use the Absent Partner Routine intentionally. Often it just happens when nobody bothers to clarify the situation. Either way, the results are the same—some experience and little progress. If your time is valuable, find out as soon as you can.

Finding out if a person can decide is as easy as asking.
"Are you the one who will hire the band for the prom?"
"Can you authorize a weekend pass?"
"Can you cancel this parking ticket?"
"If we reach an agreement, can you sign the contract?"

If they say no, politely find out who can, and arrange to contact that person.

In some situations you must deal with people who can't make the decision. If you must, you must, but when you know their authority is limited, you can save your best shots for those who can decide.

Can They Use What You Have To Offer?

If you plan to offer money in exchange for goods or services, you can usually arrange an exchange—if you offer enough. When you are offering goods, services, favors or other nonmonetary things, however, you'd better do some more checking.

Calling on apartment house owners offering airplane engines for sale would be useless. The owners could decide to buy, but they would have no use for the product.

Good sales people do preliminary research or *prospecting* to find people and organizations who can probably use the goods or services they offer. Then if that person or organization cannot use what they have to offer, they excuse themselves and find someone who can. By doing this they save time, and they also avoid dealing with refunds, bad will, and even lawsuits which can come out of selling something the customer can't use.

In some situations people might do things because they like you, it makes them feel good, or they don't have anything else to do at the moment. Responses depend on the situation, and it doesn't hurt to ask a likely prospect.

If you need a specific response from a specific person, and that person cannot use what you have to offer, you have a choice to make. Either come up with something that person can use, or shift your sights to a TARGET which involves someone who can use what you have to offer.

Can They Do What You Want Them To?

Kevin Able applied for a position as director of marketing with Bullock Manufacturing, Inc. The president and founder of the company, Seth Bullock, can make the decision, and he can certainly use Kevin's talents to market his product, buggy whips. The snag here is that Seth has not sold many buggy whips since 1937—nor will he sell any in the future—so he can't pay the $40,000 a year Cal wants.

A lot of people hire people or take jobs or buy products that don't work out. Usually they could have done a little checking and saved a lot of trouble. Some people might want to help you reach your TARGET, but they may not be able to. If Kevin Able had checked Bullock's Dun and Bradstreet ratings or talked with people who know the firm, he would never have applied.

Will They Do What They Agree To?

"You can depend on her."
"His word is his bond."
Before you go through the process of reaching an agreement, you should be reasonably sure of two things:
    1. That you will do what you will agree to, and
    2. That people you deal with will do what they agree to.

Being *able* to do something is one thing, actually doing it is another. Your TARGET with this step is to arrive at mutually-beneficial results. Would you go to a theater, wait in line, and pay for a ticket if they wouldn't let you in to see the movie?

That situation is highly improbable, but similar things happen all the time. People do take money with no intention of delivering what they agreed to. Others do contract for goods or services with no intention of paying, or take jobs with no intention of working. So we have credit bureaus, job references, and other means of checking up. These can only tell you what happened in the past, but people do tend to repeat old patterns, so they can be useful in helping you avoid the disappointment and frustration of getting an agreement but no results.

Many alcoholics and people with other chemical dependencies become experts at convincing friends and relatives that they have "straightened out and will never do those terrible things again." Then they repeat the pattern of doing the terrible things and convincing others they won't do it again.

Some people who are not chemically dependent behave the same way. Compare people's promises with their performance over a period of time. Despite the old saying, "Actions speak louder than words," sometimes the words come so loudly and so fast that we can forget to notice the actions—or lack of action.

Our society runs on trust. We trust people to do what they claim they will. There are implied warranties that products will measure up to certain standards. Businesses expect people to pay their bills. Usually that happens, and society keeps on running. Sometimes it doesn't happen, and people get disturbed. Accidents can happen, checks do get lost in the mail, and a dog probably did eat somebody's homework. But a pattern of too many accidents is no accident. Remember the old saying, "Fool me once, shame on you. Fool me twice, shame on me."

When we have no past records or experiences to refer to, we take calculated risks. When you do, be alert. Finley Peter Dunne (Mr. Dooley) said, "Trust everyone, but cut the cards."

What's In It for Them?

As they watched the farmer bringing feed to the feedlot, one steer said to another, "I keep thinking there must be something in this for him."

Michael LeBoef put it this way, "What gets rewarded gets done." Robert Heinlein was more cynical: "The greatest productive force is human selfishness." Any way you look at it, humans usually do things because there is something in it for them. And they want the value of what they get to be equal to or greater than what they have to give. When this happens they think they have a fair deal. When they have to give more than they get, they think they have an unfair, or rotten, deal.

Fair deals depend on the people involved and the circumstances. People do not value things the same. An expert collector might be willing to pay much more for a china cup and saucer than their price at a garage sale—or much less. That collector may offer less, if she thinks the price is too high, but she is not likely to offer more if it is too low. The deal is fair when both parties like the price.

Money, however, is just one of many tangible and intangible things which might motivate people to help you hit your TARGETS. Some of them might surprise you, so take nothing for granted. Investigate everyone.

By tuning in to her customers' wants, Dolores Olsen had sales totals among the highest in her company within five months of joining the firm. Selling cosmetics to retailers, Dolores developed a good relationship with her customers. She would often help them rearrange their displays, stock their shelves, and otherwise respond to their needs.

However, Dolores' district manager had other priorities. To him, doing the paper work done correctly, getting it in on time, and sticking to a rigid schedule were more important than high sales and happy customers. He fired her right after her six-month review. Nobody said it has to make sense.

Dolores made a choice. She chose—although not consciously—to please her customers rather than her boss. What could she do about it? Pay more attention to the manager's messages, find out what he really wanted, and figure out how—or *if*— she could help him reach his objectives and hit her own TARGET at the same time.

Some children—and grownups, too—do weird and obnoxious things to get attention. When parents realize that's what their kids want, they can give more attention to desirable behavior and hit their TARGET of having happier, better-behaved kids.

A corner office, a personal secretary, a company car, and other symbols of power and prestige are attractive to some people. Others don't care about them.

To find out what people want, you can use the same steps you use to define your own TARGETS. Ask what they want, get it in a positive frame and refine it. Of course circumstances vary, so you must make the best of the time available and your relationship with the other person.

IBM sales people are trained to be problem solvers for their clients, and they must not say anything about their services until they have found out exactly what the clients need.

Lee Iacocca wrote, "If a guy wanted a red convertible, of course that's what you sold him. But many customers didn't really know what they wanted, and part of the salesman's job was to help them find out."

At least those salesmen knew the customer wanted a car. What does a car represent to that person? Status? Comfort? Style? Freedom? Dependence on foreign oil? Some people even think of an automobile as a means of getting from one place to another.

Though you might not be selling cars—you may not be "selling" anything—the same principles still apply. When people don't know what they want, you may have to help them find out. Chapter 3 has some clues. Find out what "it" will do for them. Find out what they want to avoid.

Carrots and Sticks. Some people driving horse-drawn wagons used carrot-and-stick propulsion. They would tie a carrot to the end of a long pole and dangle the carrot in front of the horse, just out of reach. The horse, wanting the tasty snack, would move toward the carrot. They would also carry a stick. In case the carrot didn't work, they would whack or prod, and the horse would move away from the stick.

Some people move toward good things. They are attracted by goals and rewards. Some people move away from bad things. They steer clear of trouble and avoid punishment. Most of us do both to some extent, but be aware of this contrast. For example, a manager might reward Gary by offering a bonus and reward Jerry by not withholding the bonus.

Ask questions until you have a clear idea of what people want and whether they prefers carrots or sticks. Then feed back your impressions and notice the responses. When the nonverbal signals indicate that you are ON TARGET, you know what that person wants. Or do you?

What Do They Really Want?

Stopped at a stop sign you see a car approaching from your left with its right-turn signal blinking. What do you do? (A) Drive through the intersection, because obviously the car will turn right, or (B) Wait until you get other signals, such as slowing down and turning wheels, to confirm the turn signal?

A blinking turn signal may say, "I want to turn left," but by itself it's not enough evidence to justify risking life, limb and property. Get confirmation.

In any situation calling for expending large amounts of resources, it is a good idea to dig deeper—to confirm the signals you receive. Is that what the person *really* wants. Use the "Get into it" approach from Chapter 6.

With other people you might want to use a hypothetical situation, something like this:

1. Describe their TARGET as you understand them, and notice their nonverbal responses.
2. Say, "Think about how it will be to actually be in that situation. Is that exactly the way you want it to be?"
3. If it is, fine. If not, ask what needs to be done to make it right.
4. Keep at it until everything seems to feel right.

Relate Their TARGETS to Yours

With your TARGET and the other person's TARGET you have two important pieces of information—two points of view. Now you need one more—the relationship between the two. To get that perspective you can mentally step back, or climb up, so you see both TARGETS at the same time. Are they far apart? Close together? Do they overlap? What do they have in common?

Phil Mundy wants to take a trip to the Smoky Mountains during his two-week vacation this summer, and his wife Gloria wants to take that time to travel to Washington, D.C. They have two positions. What is their relationship?

It is a good idea to start with what they have in common. Phil and Gloria have a few things in common. Each wants to travel for two weeks, and each wants to go to the southeastern United States. If you look on a map you can see the location of each TARGET.

Unfortunately, for Phil and Gloria anyway, the Smoky Mountains and Washington, D. C. will never get any closer to each other. Fortunately, their points of view can get closer.

Whether the subject is labor relations, disarmament, trade, real estate, salaries, marriage or any other matter, negotiating parties need at least one point of common interest. Otherwise, there is no reason to negotiate. Those points can be fuzzy at first, as long as they get the parties into the same ball park.

If you have carefully qualified the other people in your venture, you must have some things in common—some points where your TARGETS overlap. With three points of view you can compare your perspective, the other party's perspective, and a broader overview which includes them both. With this information you can tell what it takes to hit two TARGETS with one shot.

Two TARGETS with One Shot

To complete the process, you need to figure out how hitting the other party's TARGET will also hit yours. Sometimes a solution is obvious, and sometimes it seems impossible. It may be impossible, but hang in there for a while. You may be surprised.

When I want gasoline for my car, I drive to a place with gas pumps where the people want to sell gasoline. Our TARGETS overlap, so we make a deal. That's easy. I hardly need to think.

Some situations do require thinking. Edward de Bono has written about what he calls *lateral thinking*, which is useful for solving unusual problems. Lateral thinking is done by deliberately avoiding point-to-point logical thinking. One way to do this is to turn your attention to the desired result and work backward. For example, people used to pay cash for most things. Then people wanting to sell big-ticket items came up with installment buying, and we can buy more things sooner.

Another approach to creatively combining two TARGETS for a single shot is to carefully consider all the aspects of the situation—your TARGET, the other party's TARGET, the relationship between the two, and any other pertinent information. Then forget it. Your mind is working behind the scenes, and it will process this information along with the rest. A little later you will have a plan.

Selling ice boxes to Eskimos has long been used as an example of an impossible task. After all, Eskimos have more than enough ways to keep things cold. That "impossible" task has been done, however, by a person who thought about how an ice box could fit the needs of people in a cold climate. An ice box is an insulated container which can keep cold in, and it can also keep cold out. The Eskimos found the ice boxes useful for keeping things from freezing.

Is It Worth It?

The Law of Supply and Demand says when supply exceeds demand, prices go down, and when demand exceeds supply, prices go up. With any TARGET of yours, you are in charge of demand. You decide if something is worth the price you have to pay.

When you figure out how you and the other party can both hit your TARGET with one shot, you know what you will have to do to get the result you want. You can estimate the amount of time, money, heavy lifting, emotional strain, or other type of payment you will have to make. The result is worth the price when you are willing to pay it.

If your plan is not worth the price, go back a few steps. Either modify your TARGET to accommodate the people you're dealing with, or find others who want something you can afford.

It's A Good Deal

When you have a plan with a price you are willing to pay, put it into effect. Join "their" team, and let them know it. Act appropriatly for the circumstances. It may be useful to say, "I'm on your side. I want you to reach your goal, and I have a plan to do that." Sometimes it is better to let your actions say that for you.

In 1978 a young woman wanted to sample some chocolate, intending to buy about three hundred pounds for a new business. She called a large chocolate company, and the salesman she talked with told her to call back when she was ready to buy ten thousand pounds. She called another large chocolate company, and within a short time its salesman was in her shop with samples. He joined her team then. In 1987 that same woman, as CEO of Mrs. Fields' Cookies, bought more than seven million dollars' worth of chocolate from his company.

When they realize you are acting in their behalf, most people will respond favorably. Some may be suspicious, especially those who have been struggling with what they believe is a "dog-eat-dog world." When you get to Chapter 11, you'll find steps to counteract suspicion and other unfavorable responses.

Sincerity

George Burns has been quoted as saying the key to acting is "sincerity. If you can fake that, you've got it made."

The problem with faking sincerity is that it requires such skilled acting that you are better off with the real thing.

In an episode of *The Paper Chase* Professor Kingsfield gave his Contract Law class a special assignment. The class was divided into ten teams, and each team had to find the answers to ten questions. Intense competition soon developed, because time and reference books were limited. As the deadline approached, the students realized that every team could not answer every question. About the same time they also realized there was no rule against cooperating, so they began making agreements to exchange answers. The ten teams became one.

And that was the real assignment: to work out mutually-beneficial contracts. And the only way anyone could pass was to work together so that everybody passed.

The Crawford Consideration

According to his peers, Crawford Clark is a fine salesman, and his record supports that opinion. Crawford said, "Whenever I make a call, I stop just before going into someone's office and think, 'My goal for this call is to have whatever comes out of it be in this person's best interest.' That sort of relaxes me and gets me off on the right foot."

Crawford's system refines many of the ideas in this book into gold. If you use this *Crawford Consideration* before every significant meeting, conversation, phone call and other communicating situation, you can bring about an definite improvement in the kinds of results you get. Here are some things using it can do for you.

- It gives you a reachable goal.
- It relaxes you, removes pressure.
- It helps put you in a RESOURCEFUL ATTITUDE.
- It reflects in your NONVERBAL SIGNALS.
- It helps build MUTUAL TRUST.
- It puts you on their team.
- It helps you avoid several TRAPS.

60 • TARGET ON RESULTS •

Team Review

Find out who the key people are—the ones who can make decisions and take actions that let you hit your TARGET.
Find out if they
  Can decide on the matter and act on it,
  Can use what you have to offer,
  Can do what you want them to, and
  Will do what they agree to.
Find out what those people's TARGETS are.
Develop a plan to hit their TARGETS and yours at the same time.
Decide whether carrying out that plan is worth the time, energy or money it may cost
If it is, join the side of the key people and use your plan to hit their TARGETS.

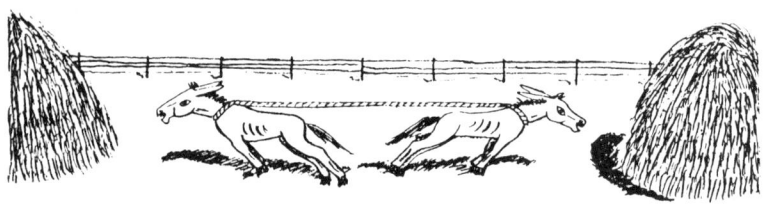

> These hieroglyphics have evidently a meaning. If it is systematic, I have no doubt we shall get to the bottom of it.
> *Sherlock Holmes*

> I see no more than you, but I have trained myself to notice what I see.
> *Sherlock Holmes*

8

TURN TO KEY CLUES

You're getting warmer with each step. But as other people get involved with your TARGET, how will you know whether you are ON TARGET or off base?

"Getting warmer" is a term from a game you may have played as a child. In the game one player hides an object, and another player seeks it. As the seeker gets closer to the object, the hider says, "You're getting warmer," and when the seeker gets farther away from it, the hider says, "You're getting cooler." When the hider says, "You're hot!" the seeker is ON TARGET.

If everyone we deal with played this game, we could have clear indicators—like the signs on interstate highways—to let us know we are getting closer, or when to turn. But how many employers, employees, friends, relatives, customers and others would tell us we're getting warmer or cooler?

Actually, the words aren't necessary. Whether we intend to or not, we all send 'warmer' and 'cooler' messages. Human beings are wired so their mental and emotional activities are reflected in some kind of outward expression or behavior. When you read them accurately, these signals can speed you to your TARGET by keeping you on course, by telling you when you hit your TARGET, or miss it.

Radar

When people show an unusual ability to anticipate others' behavior, we sometimes say they have built-in radar. Even if you don't seem to be one of those people, you can improve your

CONCENTRATE ON YOUR TARGET

At the 1932 Olympic Games Antonius Lemberkovits of Hungary hit nothing but 10's in the Small-bore Rifle, Prone, event. He would have won the gold medal, except that he got no score for one shot which hit the bull's eye of someone else's target.

With an AM radio you can hear several stations. Other receivers pick up short wave, citizens band, amateur, television, police, telephone, military, aviation, and satellite channels. The air is full of electronic signals, and with proper equipment we can receive the ones we want and make sense of them.

When you communicate with any person, you will be flooded with signals, most of which are unrelated to your TARGET. You have no electronic tuner to filter out the irrelevant signals, so you must do it yourself. You can do that and avoid filtering out the important signals by concentrating on your TARGET. Any time you wonder what to do, play back your mental tape and see, hear, and feel what you want to accomplish.

LOOK AND LISTEN FOR SIGNALS

We can quickly get overloaded with information, so we need to sort it out and focus on the information related to our TARGETS.

When you are alert, you notice things you might otherwise ignore. With a TARGET in mind, you are more likely to notice things related to that TARGET. You will be more apt to notice that you are warm or cool when you can recognize the signals.

Coded Messages

Some messages can be taken at face value. Whether they come as spoken words, written words, or behavior, these message mean just what they say.

When we see or hear words like these we know we are

hot	or	*cold.*
"You've been promoted."		"You're fired."
"I'll take it."		"I don't want it."
"Come in."		"Go away."
"A+"		"F"

We can also get clear nonverbal messages, such as

> Nodding the head "yes"
> Shaking the head "no"
> Shrugging shoulders "I don't know"
> Finger to lips "quiet"
> Hand beckoning "come here"
> Hand up, palm out "stop"

When people such as pay-TV operators, computer programmers, and secret agents want only certain people to know what their messages are, they send scrambled or coded signals. Scrambled TV signals are easy to recognize, and so are many coded messages. But some codes are cleverly disguised to look or sound like plain, clear messages. They say one thing, but to those who have the key they say something else.

Many times we mistake coded messages for plain ones, and when we realize a message is coded, we often use the wrong key to decode it. This applies to words and to the whole range of nonverbal signals.

The handbook for volunteers at the 1987 Pan American Games in Indianapolis contained this paragraph.

> Realize that gestures can be significant. Hand motions which are innocent in one culture may be offensive in another. Keep your hands relatively still and refrain from pointing—instead use wide arm motions, turning your head in the desired direction. Avoid scratching your nose, indicating the number two by holding up two fingers, or making the thumbs up or the "OK" sign.

People seldom deliberately code or disguise their words or behaviors. Even so, we can, and often do, miss, disregard, or misinterpret those signals. Doing this can lead us into traps, which are discussed in the next chapter. Here let's consider the signals as they relate to setting up and reaching a TARGET.

We operate under these conditions:

- There is more information available than we can use.
- Some information relates to our TARGETS, and most of it doesn't.
- Any human message has many elements—behavior and, sometimes, words.
- A message has no meaning except as it relates the person who sends it and a particular situation.

The good news is that you can get the information you need by using your built-in radar. You had it all the time, though you may have forgotten it. Most of us let our radar get rusty from lack of use after we developed the ability to use words and other symbols for communicating. Your radar still works, but you may need to check the manual, polish and tune up the equipment, and test the system to get it running smoothly again.

A Brief Radar Manual

Sherlock Holmes found a bullet hole the police had overlooked.
"'By George!' cried the inspector. 'How did you ever see that?'
"'Because I looked for it.'"
Holmes looked for that bullet hole because he had evidence that it must be there. The signals that indicate you are warm or cool must be there, too, and they can guide you to your TARGET when you remember to look and listen for them.

Be Careful, It Might be a Trap

Agatha Christie described some common human characteristics in this dialogue from *The Mysterious Mr. Quin.*

> "You make me see things that I ought to have seen all along—that I actually have seen—but without knowing that I saw them."
> "It sounds deuced complicated," said Colonel Monkton.
> "Not really," said Mr. Quin. "The trouble is that we are not content to see things—we will tack the wrong interpretation onto the things we see."

Not noticing and misinterpreting will come up again in Chapter 9 as traps to avoid. But here are some ways to keep safe in this chapter as you venture into Nonverbal Territory.

1. Take things in order and avoid jumping to conclusions.
2. Be aware that people send nonverbal signals
3. Know where to look and listen for useful signals
4. Find out which signals relate to your TARGET by collecting and comparing clues from the person involved so you can recognize the signals which indicate you are ON TARGET.
5. Conclude that a particular signal, or combination of signals, means something *only* after you have evaluated enough evidence from the appropriate person in the appropriate circumstances.

Until you have enough clues to decode the message, you will be safer to act as if every signal has no meaning at all. This may seem to contradict the "body language" books and articles which imply that the language of the body is just as precise as the language of words. That may be, but a Citicorp television commercial says, "Ask every American the meaning of *success*, and you won't get the same answer twice." That's almost 250,000,000 meanings for one word.

Bandler, Ekman, Grinder, Hall, Knapp, and others who have studied the subject, point out that the meaning of any behavior, or word, depends on who is doing it and in what situation.

Isolate and Investigate

You have probably noticed that people don't freeze in position to allow you to take in all the signals they may be sending. However, by using techniques similar to those used with video tape—the isolation camera, and the freeze frame—you can soon get up to speed. If you did it when you were an infant, surely you can do it now.

When he was developing his basketball skills, Bill Russell would watch players on the court, and he later wrote,

> Every time one of them would make one of the moves I liked, I'd close my eyes just afterward and try to see the play in my mind. In other words, I'd try to create an instant replay on the inside of my eyelids. Usually I'd catch only part of a particular move the first time I tried this... But the next time I saw the move I'd catch a little more of it, so that soon I could call up a complete picture.

To get acquainted with nonverbal clues, you will probably find it easier to investigate small parts, then put them together as they become more familiar. First, you will need to pay attention to things you may be ignoring. Read the next few paragraphs to find out the best sources of valuable clues which can let you know whether you are warm or cool. Then spend a day or so focused on, or tuned to, just one of them. By the time you get to all of them, your radar should be in good shape.

CLUES TO LOOK FOR

When most people look at others, they usually notice something like this:

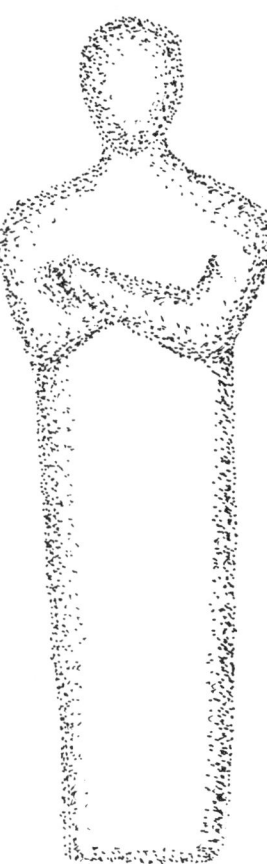

As we start to focus on small areas, we discover fascinating things which we may have known, but forgotten.

Let's start at the top with

the *Forehead.*
Is it relaxed?
Tense?
Furrowed?
Frowning?
Are eyebrows raised?
Lowered?

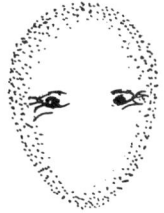

Eyes. Are they
Wide open?
Closed?
Half closed?
Looking at you?
Looking away?
Looking up?
Looking down?
To the side?
Dilated?
Blinking?
How often?
Are muscles
Relaxed?
Tense?

68 • TARGET ON RESULTS

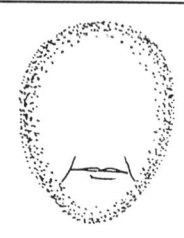

Mouth	*Nose/Cheeks/Jaw*
Relaxed?	Relaxed?
Tense?	Tense?
Lips pursed?	Nose wrinkled?
Smile?	Nostrils flared?
Frown?	Jaw clenched?
Lip size?	Cheeks blushing?
Lip color?	Pale?

Head. Is it straight? Cocked? Leaning forward? Leaning Back? Nodding? Shaking?

Neck. Is it relaxed? Tense? What color is it? Can you see the pulse beat? Swallowing?

Shoulders. Are they relaxed? Tense? Raised? Back? Forward? Slumped? Do they move with breathing?

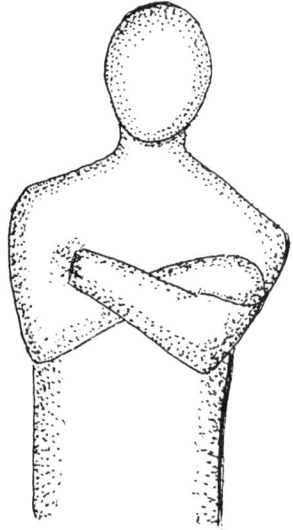

Hands and Arms. Are they relaxed? Tense? Folded? Hands clenched? Open? Still? Moving? How fast? What pattern?

Upper Body. Is it relaxed? Tense? What position is it in?

Lower Body. Is it relaxed? Tense? Standing? Sitting? Legs crossed? Foot or Leg moving? What pattern? How fast?

Breathing. Is it steady? Irregular? Rapid? Slow? Deep? Shallow? In the chest? at the diaphragm? In the abdomen?

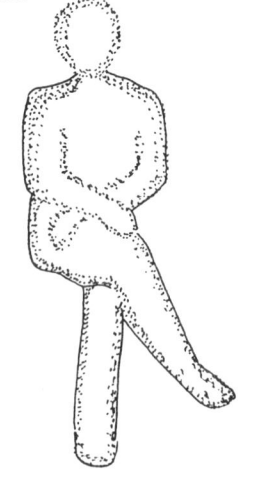

Some signals, such as posture, walking and gestures, can involve several, or all, parts of the body.

Posture. What is the position of the head, shoulders, torso, arms, and legs? Are they relaxed? Tense? Erect? Slumped? Spread out? Drawn in?

Walking. Is it fast or slow? Smooth? Jerky? Which part of the body leads? Nose? Chin? Chest? Pelvis?

Gestures. Are they smooth? Jerky? Tense? Relaxed? Restricted? Expansive? Slow? Fast? Seldom? Often?

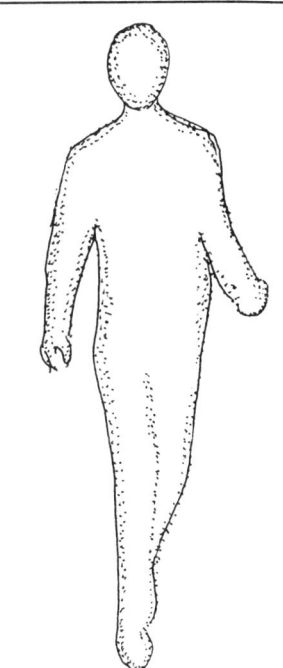

After you pay close attention to each of these areas for a while individually, they come together, and people begin to look more like this:

CLUES TO LISTEN FOR

When people speak, they do more than project words. They also tell you about their moods, attitudes, and thought processes through what Knapp calls vocal cues. And he says those cues can be more than *how* something is said. "Frequently they are *what* is said." Notice these clues.

Volume. Is the voice loud? Soft? Moderate? Varying? Does the volume increase? Decrease?

Pitch. Is the voice high? Low? Medium?

Inflection. Does the pitch vary? Does it stay the same?

Rate of Speech. Is it fast? Slow? Moderate? Does it get faster? Slower?

Rhythm. Is it steady? Irregular? Are there hesitations? Pauses?

Quality. Is the voice harsh? Pleasant? Nasal? Resonant? Flat? Whining? Shrill? Melodious?

After you spend some time tuned in to each of these clues, you will develop an ear for the ones which relate to your TARGETS.

But What Does it Mean?

It seems there were two psychiatrists...

As that old joke suggests, it is possible to over-interpret simple responses. But we are even more likely to miss important information which is right in front of us.

John Watson, a scientist in Douglas Adams' *So Long, and Thanks for all the Fish*, said,

A scientist must be absolutely like a child. If he sees a thing, he must say that he sees it, whether it is what he thought he was going to see or not. See first, think later, then test. But always see first. Otherwise you will only see what you were expecting.

That's a good way to think about it. Blips on a radar screen mean nothing until an operator recognizes their patterns. The visual and vocal clues you detect with your built-in radar mean nothing until you can recognize their patterns.

UNCOVER KEYS BY COMPARING

A fad a few years ago was to wear a ring with a large oval stone which changed colors to match the wearer's mood. People don't wear mood rings any more, so we have to look at the body and listen to the voice to get the information we want.

To stay ON TARGET, you need to know about a person's mood or state of mind which is most likely to lead to that TARGET. You also need reliable signals to show and tell you that person is in that mood.

Your TARGET might require a serious mood, and in some cases a joking mood would be more desirable. Here is a sample of some possible 'warm' and 'cool' moods.

Warm	*Cool*
Agreeable	Opposed
Attentive	Distracted
Happy	Unhappy
Joking	Serious
Pleased	Displeased
Receptive	Resistant
Responsive	Unresponsive
Serious	Joking
Understanding	Confused

People tend to repeat certain patterns of behavior in similar situations—especially patterns they don't notice. Over a period of time other people can recognize those patterns, usually by accident. By knowing what to look and listen for, you can do it on purpose—more quickly and accurately.

The key to the warm or cool code is comparison.

Thinking of a person she does not like, Billie Filmore has a pleasant smile on her face. Thinking of someone she likes, Billie has a broad smile on her face. Under the same circumstances,

August Grimm has a frown on his face, but the frown is less intense when he thinks of someone he likes.

People tend to repeat behavior patterns, so you can get reliable signals if you understand that they repeat their *own* patterns, not someone else's, and that they may have different patterns for different situations. *Therefore*, it is essential that you have hard evidence before making any judgements on important matters. People have been known to cause severe damage by jumping to conclusions and missing.

The key clues are the ones which change from one mood to another. This varies from person to person. One person's "angry scowl" can be another's "thoughtful consideration," so treat each person as a one-of-a-kind item. Comparing Billie's responses with August's just won't work. To get accurate information, notice how the person you must deal with looks and sounds when in the mood you want in an appropriate situation. *Compare that with the same person's signals when in other moods or situations, and notice the differences.* For example:

The face gives us much information. We have expressions like "It's written all over your face," and we have expressions like *stone face* and *poker face* which indicate a lack of expression. Even a poker face may have telltale clues, although they may be harder to detect. But, with a poker face or an open book, the key clues may not be on the face at all. Remember all the other clues. Voice, for instance, or feet. Some card players keep poker faces above the table and tap dance under it.

Past Experience

Dr. Watson wrote, "Sherlock Holmes preserved his calm professional manner until our visitor had left us, although it was easy for me, who knew him well, to see that he was profoundly excited."

Some members of President Eisenhower's staff kept very low profiles when Ike wore a brown suit. They had noticed that Eisenhower displayed his temper on those days, and it was worth avoiding.

Most wives can tell when their husbands would favor eating out. Most employees know when the boss will say yes to a request for a couple of days off.

With enough exposure to another person we seem to absorb that kind of information without realizing it. Unfortunately, we can also jump to erroneous conclusions. We often form opinions early in a relationship and act as if those opinions were accurate, so it's a good idea to check them out if you have any question about their reliability. You must be able to recognize patterns which consistently demonstrate the kind of signals you want in the situation you are concerned with.

Irene Simms made lasagna for her husband Herb every Wednesday night for twelve years. Then she overheard Herb saying his favorite food was Swiss steak.

Irene said, "I thought your favorite food was lasagna."

Herb said, "I don't really care for lasagna."

"But I've been making lasagna every Wednesday because I thought it was your favorite. You always eat it."

"I eat it because you make it. I thought it was your favorite. You make it all the time."

Those people have been acting according to faulty conclusions for twelve years. Many people do the same thing in much more serious matters.

When you don't have reliable personal experience to decode someone's messages, you can make other arrangements.

ENTICE A DEMONSTRATION

Before you entice a demonstration, decide what you want demonstrated. For example, you may need to know what someone looks and sounds like agreeing with an idea. Since it is socially strange to go into someone's office and say, "Would you show me what you look like when you agree with an idea," you might want to use a less direct approach. One way would be to bring up something from his past.

"You supported Multidirectional Interflow applied to Omniphasic Matrices, didn't you?"

"Why, yes, I did."
"How did you know it was a good idea?"

As he tells you about that experience, he will demonstrate the way he looks and sounds when he agrees with an idea.

Since you only want a message that leads to your TARGET, lead the person into an experience which requires that meaning, and she will demonstrate what the message looks and sounds like. When she does, be aware of body, eyes, face and voice, and notice what changes from one situation to another.

You can also do what lawyers do in court, propose a hypothetical situation. "Have you ever thought about an ideal computer network?" "If you had the vacation of your dreams, what would it be like?" "What's your favorite meal?"

Another way to entice a demonstration is to put the person into a situation where he must be in the mental state you want. If you want agreement, get him to agree on something—taxes, music, sports, television, restaurants. As he agrees, notice what changes. If you aren't sure, get him to disagree and notice what changes. Then go back to agreeing and check it out.

STORE KEY CLUES FOR REFERENCE

When you have identified reliable clues which indicate this person is in the mood you want, *store those key clues so you can refer to them later.* It helps if you have both seeing and hearing information. You are more likely to recognize the signals when they reach more than one of your senses.

You can use these visual and vocal clues to get information which can keep you ON TARGET and tell you when you hit, or miss, your TARGET. When you know what a person's 'warm' and 'cool' signals look and sound like, those signals become part of what you will see, hear and feel when you hit your TARGET. Store them in your memory, and, when you communicate with that person, say and do things which produce 'warm' signals..

You will get signals. They may be the ones you were aiming for, and they may be something else. Either way, you can use them as feedback to get, or keep, you ON TARGET. Do this by comparing the signals you actually get from that person, the feedback, with the responses you have stored for reference. This subject comes up in Chapter 12. When you get cool signals, you need to adjust your approach as discussed in Chapter 13. And

76 • TARGET ON RESULTS •

when you get "warm" signals, you are ON TARGET, and we get to that in Chapter 14.

Key Clue Review

Everybody sends signals which can let us know when we are on course and when we get to our TARGETS. To use these signals effectively, we need to know what to look and listen for. These signals are unique for each individual, so we need clues to what a particular person looks and sounds like in that situation when responding the way you want. To sort out these clues,

    C - Concentrate on your TARGET.
    L - Look and listen for signals.
    U - Uncover the key clues by comparing signals from the same person in different moods or attitudes.
    E - Entice a demonstration of the state of mind you need.
    Ask about a past situation when they were in that mood,
    Talk about a hypothetical situation to bring it on, or
    Set up an actual situation calling for that mood.
    As they demonstrate the desired mood, notice which visual and vocal clues change and how.
    S - Store the Key Clues for Reference.

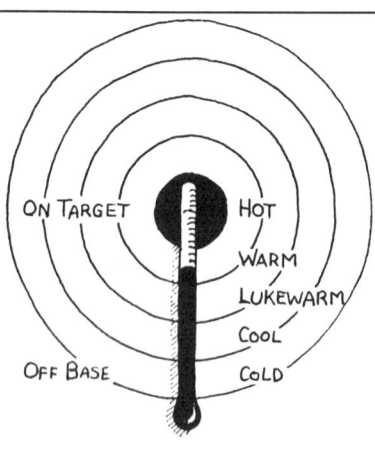

PART 3

RESULTS ON TARGET

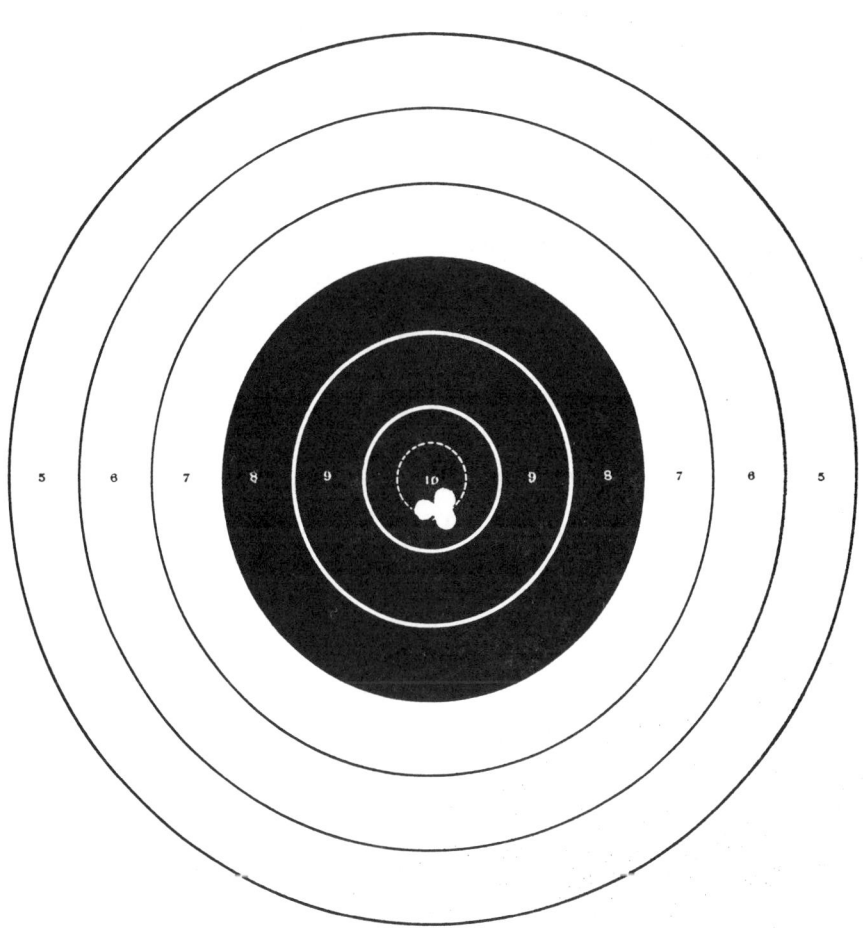

> I would begin here. I would
> make something happen.
> *Louis L'amour*

RESULTS ON TARGET

With a clear TARGET, you are well on your way to getting the result you want. When you set up a target on a rifle range, you are just beginning. You still have to aim, fire, check, and adjust. When you set up a personal or business TARGET, you may not need to do anything else. You may not even have time to do anything else. I have often thought of results I wanted, then had those results before I did anything else to get them.

Many times, however, you need to take more steps. The next six chapters give you some positive steps for getting along with people and for making your TARGETS easier to reach.

R- Recognize And Avoid Traps.

Too many of us make a habit of shooting ourselves in the foot—of defeating our own purposes by falling into traps which are often disguised as "the thing to do." We can fall into the same trap many times and not realize that is what keeps us from our TARGETS. This chapter points out how you can recognize some common traps and what you can do to avoid them.

E - Establish Resourceful Attitudes.

Attitudes play a major part in getting results. A person with ability and a confident, resourceful attitude has an excellent chance of hitting a TARGET. A person with an I-can't-do-it attitude usually can't, even with superior ability.

You can establish these attitudes by retrieving them from your past, by taking on the physical aspects of the desired attitudes, by mentally rehearsing, and by actual practice.

When you communicate with other people, it is a good idea for them to be in receptive, resourceful attitudes. This chapter also gives you techniques for leading others into these attitudes.

S - Support The Process With Mutual Trust.

Your top priority in dealing with others should be to make sure you have enough mutual trust to accomplish your purpose.

Do you trust them to carry out any agreements you want. If not, either modify your TARGET or deal with somebody else.

People like and trust people who are like themselves in some way. You can increase others' trust in you by following some of their verbal and nonverbal signals, such as

dress	posture
movements	breathing
rate of speech	pitch
pet words and phrases	volume
see, hear, or feel language	

You can also build trust in others when they sense you are willing to support them in reaching their TARGET.

U - Use Your Clues.

When you are communicating to get a particular result, the clues you have identified can be a valuable indicator of your progress. Pay attention to the signals you get from others and use them to direct what you do.

L - Loosen Up — Take Another Approach.

If at first you don't succeed, do something else. If the clues say "cooler" or "cold," do something to get back ON TARGET.

Check for resourceful attitudes, mutual trust, traps, and acknowledged objections

Some useful techniques are: using *and* rather than *but*, hypothetical situations, surprise, and stories.

T - Take Yes For An Answer.

When the signals show or tell that you have the result you want, stop what you are doing — even though you may have planned much more — and take the next step.

Be prepared to accept something better than you expected.

S - Step This Way.

This chapter recaps the steps in Part 2 and Part 3, and gives you a check list to use to keep ON TARGET.

RECOGNIZE AND AVOID TRAPS

> Be careful, it may be a trap.
> *Movie Dialogue*

> Never underestimate the degree
> of possible misunderstanding.
> *Philip Lesly*

9
RECOGNIZE AND AVOID TRAPS

In Chapter 3 we met Jim Hawkins, who found the map to *Treasure Island,* and his friends, Dr. Livesy and Squire Trelawney. Once these three saw the map, their attention focused on the treasure, and they started noticing many things related to finding it. Unfortunately, they also ignored some vital information which could have kept them out of a dangerous trap. In those days the only way to get to an island was by sea, so Squire Trelawney went to Bristol, the nearest port, bought a schooner and went about acquiring a crew. By a stroke of luck the man he hired as cook was a great help in finding a crew in a short time.

This cook, a pleasant fellow named Long John Silver, "lost a leg in the service of his country." When young Hawkins heard this, he wondered about the "seafaring man with one leg" whom the late captain had feared. But Jim lost his suspicions when he met the man, a delightful chap—not at all like the dirty, rough-talking pirates whom Jim had heard threaten the captain.

When they got to Treasure Island, however, Jim and his friends discovered they had more than Captain Flint's treasure map. They also had most of his pirate crew, thanks to Long John Silver, the fiercest of the pirates.

Squire Trelawney and Jim Hawkins knew pirates were after the treasure. They even had a description of the chief pirate. But they had a fixed idea of what pirates look and sound like, so they lulled themselves into a false sense of security and walked into a trap.

The best way to deal with traps, obstacles, and self-inflicted wounds which can delay or prevent your reaching your TARGET is to avoid them. In fact, An Wang, founder and chairman of Wang Laboratories, has this advice for succeeding in business: avoid "shooting yourself in the foot. If you can keep from shooting yourself in the foot long enough, people start calling you a genius."

Of course most people would not fall into traps, if they realized they were traps. So the first step in avoiding traps is to *recognize them*. This may not be easy to do. You could have as much trouble as Jim Hawkins did if you have come to believe that some of these detours and dead ends are actually the main road. This chapter posts warnings so you can be alert for the tell-tale signs.

Types of Traps

We limit ourselves unnecessarily, even prevent ourselves from hitting our own TARGET, by falling into traps like these:

- Expecting others to respond the way we expect
- Ignoring the signals we get from others.
- Misinterpreting the clues we get

EXPECTING

> People differ. Some object to the fan dancer, others to the fan.
> *Elizabeth W. Spalding*

People are pretty much alike—except when they aren't.

Watch people in a shopping mall. How many look alike or dress alike? You'll see similarities, but are any exactly alike?

Our thoughts and actions are influenced by information we have been storing since before birth, information which can only come from our own experiences. No two people can have identical experiences, so they can't have identical thoughts or behaviors.

We do share some experiences with others, and "birds of a feather flock together." We tend to associate with people we have something in common with, and we notice the similarities. This leads us into the trap of believing (1) that people are pretty much alike, (2) that they will think and act the same in all situations, and (3) that they will think and act the same as we would.

Many of the specific traps pointed out in this chapter have to do with expecting others to behave the way we expect them to behave. Often they will, but if you are aiming for an important TARGET, you would be wise to have specific information about the people involved. People do tend to follow old patterns of behavior, but the patterns are their own, not anyone else's.

IGNORING SIGNALS

> The human eye has a readiness for patterns. Much is not seen simply because the mind is blind, not the eyes.
>
> *Louis L'Amour*

Every day we are exposed to more information than we can possibly pay conscious attention to, so we ignore a lot of it. We can get along without most of it, but once in a while we miss a vital piece of information right in front of our eyes or ears. As a result we can miss opportunities, or we can get into trouble.

The great detective, Sherlock Holmes, has been popular for more than a hundred years. His most notable accomplishment was paying attention to clues that others overlooked. Many clues available to us come in the form of nonverbal signals. They can be quite obvious — to someone trained to notice.

MISINTERPRETING

> The trouble is that we are not content to see things — we will tack the wrong interpretation onto the things we see.
>
> *Harley Quin*

Holmes knew how to interpret clues he found. Many of us notice clues, both verbal and nonverbal, but still miss the message. We have been led to believe that words, postures and movements have specific, standard meanings. Unfortunately, those meanings vary from time to time and from person to person.

Safety

On a rifle range the rule is Safety First. People are extremely conscious of the dangers, and as a result, very few accidents happen there. Accidents happen when people don't know of the dangers or forget about them. "He shot himself in the foot" is as much a part of our language as "But what went wrong?" and "I didn't know it was loaded."

TRAPS TO AVOID

Golfers know what and where the trees, lakes and other hazards are on the course, and still they hit balls into the sand and lose them in the woods. Some people actually make a good living selling golf balls they retrieve from water hazards.

When most people tee up their communication balls and aim for the RESULT flag on the green, they do not realize there are hazards on the course. They hit the ball, head for the green, and wonder why the balls don't show up. Lawyers, marriage counselors, psychiatrists and others make a good living retrieving these people from various traps.

Following are some ways people manage to shoot themselves in the foot and otherwise prevent themselves from succeeding. This is not a complete list of all possible traps. It is a collection of common examples of ways we defeat our own purposes by doing things we think we should be doing. Each of these traps stems from the general traps: expecting others to act as you expect them to, ignoring signals, and misinterpreting clues. By knowing about these pitfalls and pratfalls, you can get a good idea of what traps are, how they work, and how to avoid them.

TRAP 1
"How could they do that?"

Clara Martin often says, "I don't understand how they could do that. I would never think of doing something like that."

One way to get surprised, disappointed and frustrated is to expect someone else to think or act the way you would.

Actually, our values, our behavior, our response patterns are determined by our genetic code, our lifetime of experiences, and our emotional responses to those experiences. Since no two people can have the same experiences over a lifetime, expecting any two people to respond the same way to anything is extremely risky. Expecting *everybody* to respond the same way is definitely a trap.

When you realize how much others differ from you in heredity, environment, personality, and other factors it is easier to understand how they can do the unusual, weird, and bizarre things they do. They can still seem strange, but with their backgrounds, what else could they do?

Unless we realize this we can wander into the trap. People will think, talk, and act perfectly sensibly and reasonably (like we would, that is) in some situations, regarding some subjects. So we jump to a conclusion and expect them to behave just as reasonably in all situations. By expecting this, we set ourselves up for unpleasant surprises we may not be ready to handle.

Be prepared to deal with people acting in ways you would never think of. That way you will be expecting it when they do and say weird things, and if they happen to act sensibly, your surprise will be pleasant.

"They're just like us."

People get friendly when they notice the ways they are alike. They quarrel when they pay attention to their differences.

Take, for instance, two countries, The United States of America and the Union of Soviet Socialist Republics. Certain people in the USA talk as though all the people of the USSR—Russians, Ukranians, Uzbeks, Armenians, Georgians, etc.—are alike, different from us, and should be treated as enemies. Other people in the USA say the Soviet people are "just like us" and should be treated as friends. Treating people as friends is all right, and so is verifying compliance with treaties, but expecting 250,000,000 people in another society to be "just like us" is expecting too much. Even "we" are not just like us.

All people have a great number of biological and sociological similarities and a great number of personality and behavioral differences. The similarities seem to show up in large groups. So actuaries can be surprisingly accurate when they tell insurance companies how many people will have traffic accidents next year, but they can't tell who those people will be.

You can avoid this trap by remembering that each person is different from every other person in some ways and is, therefore, likely to display some peculiarities from time to time. Expect it and you can save yourself a lot of surprise and disappointment.

TRAP 2
"That wasn't what I meant/But I thought she meant..."

We send messages full of meaning, and sometimes other people take them the wrong way. What is their problem? Can't they understand English?

86 • RESULTS ON TARGET

When we want to hit specific TARGETS, the problem is not theirs, it is ours. We all put our experiences together in different ways, so the messages others receive may mean something different to them than we intended. At this point average people blame others for not understanding. Effective communicators take charge and do something others *can* understand.

Here is a short course in how people communicate.

This continues as long as these people are within sight or hearing of each other, whether they want it to or not. The critical factor in this exchange is (6), the message Jan sends in response to Dan's message (2). Despite Dan's intentions, the result of his message is found in Jan's response to it. Marshall McLuhan wrote, "More and more we turn from the content of messages to study the total effect." Bandler and Grinder said, "The meaning of any communication is the response it gets."

When we shift our focus from our intentions to the responses we get, we can do something about getting the responses/results we want. It becomes a matter of **knowing what response we want and noticing what response we get.**

We sent a message and the response was not the one we wanted. What do we do now? Send another message.

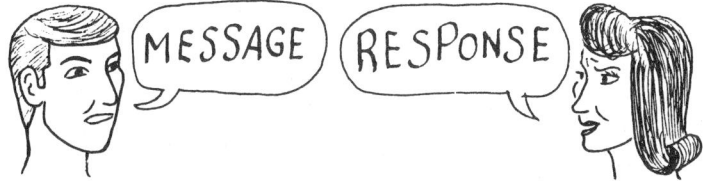

That was not another message. That was the same message, and it got the same response. We do not want that response, so we send another message, adapting it according to the responses we got.

Now we are going in the right direction. We sent a different message and got a different response. We still do not have the response we want, but we are getting warmer, so we send another message.

That's it! We have the target response, which means we have the result we want.

We got what we wanted by sending just three messages. But most people send only one. They fall into the trap of focusing on their intentions and thinking they can't do anything else.

In reality we can do many other things, and get many different responses. Pay attention to the response you get. It tells you what your message means to that person at that time.

> **TRAP 3**
> "She wouldn't listen to reason, even though I was right."

Were you ever positive you were right, had facts, figures and reasons for support, yet could not get someone else to admit she was wrong? Despite the sheer force of logic and enthusiasm fueled by absolute certainty, sometimes we cannot sway someone who is obviously wrong and refuses to change his opinion. Trying to change someone else's mind is a trap filled with quicksand, and the more we struggle, the deeper we sink. Somehow another person's stubborn resistance to "the truth" only spurs us on to more vehement arguing until we are in over our heads.

Arguing is a popular sport, and it can serve some useful purposes—as a sport. It exercises lungs, vocal cords, reasoning processes, and word selection. As a method of influencing another person's actions it is extremely inefficient, and as a method of changing someone else's mind it hardly ever works. How many times have you changed your mind when someone told you you were wrong? Even if they had good reasons.

One of Dale Carnegie's rules for winning friends and influencing people is to avoid arguments. Carnegie said to respect other people's opinions and to never tell people they are wrong. If we do, we stand a good chance of causing ill will and resentment. We can do great damage, and our chances of really winning an argument are almost zero. Charlie Chan said, "The ignorant are never defeated in an argument," and those we would argue with must be ignorant, otherwise they would agree with us. Wouldn't they?

"He won't listen to reason" usually means "he doesn't agree with me." We may give sound, logical reasons and still not persuade. Jonathan Swift wrote, "It is useless to attempt to reason a man out of a thing he was never reasoned into." That also applies to women.

Once you have set a TARGET for yourself, keep it in mind and be aware of possible detours. If you are tempted to stray from the path and fall into an argument, ask yourself which is more important, getting someone to admit you are right or hitting your TARGET? If that person refuses to admit she is wrong, what is harmed? Weigh the possible damages to your relationship with that person and the possibility of missing your TARGET against the slim possibility that you might argue or reason her into changing her mind.

Macy's department stores did quite well with the motto, "The Customer is Always Right." Tony Hoffman, in a real estate seminar on cable television, said that when negotiating the sale of a property, he would set up a situation so the other party could change or correct something in the contract. Hoffman said, "I want him to be right so I can be rich."

Edward de Bono wrote,

1. Everyone is always right
2. No one is ever right

These are not contradictory. In his own mind no one is wrong on purpose. According to his knowledge, experience, emotions and the way he looks at things a person sets up his ideas in the best possible way. One has to realize that this is the case when one is dealing with other minds. It may be obvious but it is very easy to forget. ...

Although everyone is always right within his own context this rightness is not absolute but limited to that context.

To stay out of the argument trap, argue only as recreation. The way to win an argument is to avoid it. Reason only with reasonable people on reasonable subjects. To persuade, appeal to emotions, then furnish reasons to support a person's decision to agree with you. Be aware that "everyone is always right," **AND** "no one is ever right," so be careful about investing time and energy in proving your rightness or someone else's wrongness.

TRAP 3A
"There are two sides to every question."

Jim Fagan was a radio newsman from the Midwest before he joined a Congressman's staff. When asked about his biggest surprise in Washington, Fagan said, "When I was a newsman I knew there were two sides to every question, but in Washington I quickly found out there are at least twenty-five."

When we reduce the possibilities in a situation to two, we limit our abilities to find the most desirable, effective or efficient answer to a question, solution to a problem, or path to a

TARGET. Saying it must be black or white ignores the shades of gray, and it also overlooks all the colors of the rainbow.

Many people say, "There are two sides to every question," intending to be generous by admitting someone else might have another opinion. But that pushes them into the either-or trap.

You can stay out of that trap by realizing there are a great number of possible sides to most questions, and several of them could be better than an either-or choice.

TRAP 4
"He disagrees with everything."

One day I leaped on a horse I had not ridden before, and discovered she wanted to stay with the herd. Despite my urging, she would not go forward. She would go backward, so we backed up to where I wanted to go.

Some people are contrary. They disagree with others, and if you pay attention, you might notice them disagreeing with themselves. If you say odd, they say even. But if you say, "Maybe it was even," they say, "No, it was odd."

You might notice, too, that their tendency to disagree has little to do with the subject of discussion, the point of view you offer, or the position you take. Their mission is to disagree or to point out what is wrong.

This can be a useful quality under certain circumstances. It can help you find flaws in an argument or a plan. It can help you avoid situations others might leap into to their sorrow. And it can get you into trouble.

With some people being contrary is a tendency. With others it is a way of life, a reflex action. They will spend a lot of time in wheat fields so they can go against the grain. Any reflex can have drawbacks, but this one is so easy for others to control, that you had better make sure you are going in a direction you want to. The horse had her way in that she did not go forward, but we ended up where I wanted to go.

Martin Merger found out about this contrary reflex in a workshop. The next day he was negotiating to buy Phil Merchant's business and getting nowhere. Everything Martin proposed Phil rejected. Then Martin remembered what he had heard in the workshop. He started saying things like, "Then you don't really want to sell, do you?" and "We probably couldn't agree on terms anyway." Then Phil answered, "Sure I do," and

"Of course we could." From there on it was easy. In this case Phil ended up with what he wanted, but he almost missed out by automatically disagreeing with everything.

Jane Marble's boss, Chuck Avery, automatically rejected every idea she suggested until she discovered his contrariness. Then, when Jane said things like, "You probably won't like this idea..." Chuck disagreed.

Mary Frost was a counselor who worked with people convicted of drunk driving. She had the difficult task of persuading people with drinking problems to volunteer for a treatment program. She told one man, "You probably don't see the benefits of going to treatment," and he proceeded to tell her he did see the benefits. Then he convinced her that he should go to treatment and had her call the treatment center.

When someone disagrees with you, keep in mind it might be a reflex, and notice what happens when you use some negative phrasing like, "You may not agree...," "I don't know if you want to...," or "You might not understand the benefits of...."

Mark Twain summed up the contrary response this way.

> Adam was but human—this explains it all. He did not want the apple for the apple's sake, he wanted it only because it was forbidden. The mistake was in not forbidding the serpent; then he would have eaten the serpent.

I don't know if you understand what to do when you find out a person is contrary, but we have had some examples. In these examples, the outcomes were in the contrary person's best interests, and they recognized them as such. Other incidents have not been so fortunate.

How many times have we heard this story? Parents "absolutely forbid" their daughter to see some sleezeball jerk whose most attractive feature is that her parents disapprove. The forbiddings escalate until the daughter ends up pregnant at fifteen.

Things like that happen to people who do not notice contrariness and the power of negative phrasing. Everybody loses. Any time the outcome is contrary to the interests of *any* of the parties involved, *everybody* loses.

TRAP 4A
"Not me!"

Do you have automatic contrary reactions? If you immediately said, "Not me!" check again. The quicker you denied it, the more likely you are to have an automatic contrary response. You are not likely to recognize it, especially if someone suggests you might have it.

Even if you do have it, you may not want to do something about it. But there are a couple of drawbacks to not having more choices. One is that people who find the right buttons-intentionally or accidentally—can play you like Heifetz with a Stradivarius. Another is that, when we only notice what is wrong, what is missing and what we disagree with, we miss out on the benefits of an idea, product or person. Then we find ourselves saying later, "I could have bought that stock at 15, but who could believe people would buy machines to copy pieces of paper when they already had carbon paper?"

But what can you do to avoid automatic contrary responses? You can't...unless you realize what is happening when it happens. If you need help, you could ask your friends and relatives to call those responses to your attention. They will know. Then, when you are aware of the situation, you can ask yourself what other choices you have. Could you be missing out on something useful? Is there something you have not thought of? How could this be valuable? Remember, you can still disagree, but that response is much more valuable as a choice than as a compulsion.

TRAP 5
"Look me in the eye and say that."

John T. Molloy writes that when he was a boy his grandmother caught him saying something she did not believe. She said, "Look me in the eye and say that." She told him a person could not lie while looking someone in the eye, and that a person who looked away was lying. Molloy immediately went to a mirror and practiced until he could lie while looking her in the eye.

Joan Ayer prefers visual information, and when she is talking, she wants listeners to look at her so she can see they are paying attention.

Jerry Sayer prefers feeling information, and he also talks to himself in his head. When he talks with someone, he looks down a lot to gather his thoughts.

Victor Starrett looks directly at people, constantly. After a while they begin to feel uncomfortable.

According to Knapp, eye contact can do several things:

> 1) regulating the flow of communication—opening the channels of communication and assisting in the turn-taking process; (2) monitoring feedback; (3) expressing emotions; and (4) communicating the nature of the interpersonal relationship.

These things all depend on the person and the context. Eye contact in itself has no great significance. It does not reveal lying or telling the truth. Eye contact does not even indicate paying attention. Until you have a reliable reference, the only thing you really know when a person is looking at you is...that person is looking at you. A person looking at something else, reading, or apparently catching a nap may be listening attentively to what you say. Someone looking intently into your eyes may be a million miles away and have no idea what you are talking about.

When people talk they often look away to recall and organize information. We tend to search for seeing information by looking up. ("Now let me see") Or straight ahead. We recall hearing information by moving our eyes to the side. ("That sounds interesting.") Looking down gives us a grasp of feeling information. ("I feel this will be hard, but we'll pull through.")

Pay attention to the ways people move their eyes. They may be going through some interesting thought patterns to make sense of what you are saying, or what they are about to say. Maintaining eye contact may not be the most effective way of listening. It might throw their minds out of gear.

You know what is going on, so you can regard others' eye contact, or lack of it, as part of their individual communicating patterns.

Your own eye contact, however, is another story. Most people expect it, so give them some—but not too much. People are usually comfortable in a conversation when someone looks at them about half the time. They are uncomfortable when the person does not look at them at all, and they are more uncomfortable when the person stares at them constantly. So look at people—in moderate amounts—so they feel comfortable.

> **TRAP 6**
> "Keep the change."

A young reporter was assigned to interview a local man on his 100th birthday. The reporter said, "You must have seen a lot of changes in your day," and the centenarian replied, "Yep. And I was agin every one of 'em."

According to Rodger Bailey and Ross Stewart, approximately 70 percent of the population has a negative reaction to the idea of change and to words suggesting it, like *change, new,* and *revolutionary*. You would be wise to consider the reactions of a group that large. Like any other reflex action, this one does not involve thinking, so trying to convince an old, established firm that it needs to change its corporate culture to something new and different is like digging your own quicksand traps.

The good news is that these are words, and their meanings are in the minds of the beholder. If these words do not do the job, find some that do.

John Grinder said people can tolerate changes as long as they are not labeled as such. Compare your life today with what it was ten years ago. Do you have a compact disc player, a VCR, a personal computer? Looking back, we can identify certain things which are different, although at the time nobody announced "This is a major change!" In fact, nobody announced anything, so we took it in stride. Alan Jackson said, "If somebody had told me a year ago that I would sell my business, quit drinking and smoking, and start living alone, I wouldn't have been able to face it." But nobody told him all that would happen, so he didn't have to face it. He just did it.

When you want to present ideas to people who don't like change, you can improve your chances by using better, more effective words. Like *improve, better* and *more*. Although 70 percent of the population does not like the idea of change, 65 percent of the population does like some variety and wants to improve conditions, make life better, and reach their goals more often. This is another case of "It's not what you say, it's how you phrase it." In other words, there are other words. When you propose changes, differences, and new things, 70 percent will resist the ideas, and 30 percent will be willing to listen. When you propose improving and making things better, 65 percent should be willing to listen.

Notice advertising, sales people, or people who have just discovered the latest and greatest thing which will completely change your life. Notice how many people want others to change. Parents, children, employees, employers, friends and lovers tell each other it would be great "if you would change." On *60 Minutes* Andy Rooney talked about some rather exotic how-to books he had displayed on his desk, then he said, "We are what we are, and the same things keep happening to the same people, no matter what how-to books they read." That does not really tell us much about how-to books or the people who read them, but it does tell us something about Andy Rooney. He likes things to stay the same.

To find out whether someone prefers changes or sameness, pay attention. Notice clothing, hair styles, cars and other trendy items. If they are the latest fashion, you can suspect their owners like changes. How long have they been in their job, home or relationship? If they regularly change any of those in three years or less, they probably like change in that area. On the other hand, people who do not wear the latest fashions and stay in one place seven years and more tend to dislike the idea of change.

But what about the woman who changes detergents every year and keeps the same husband for thirty years? These preferences, like others, can vary from situation to situation.

> **TRAP 7**
> **"We don't see eye-to-eye."**

In *The Odd Couple* Felix Unger, a neatness freak, and Oscar Madison, a slob, shared an apartment. Felix wanted things to look neat. Oscar didn't care what they looked like, he wanted them comfortable. Felix gave more value to what he saw. Oscar gave more value to what he felt. As a result, these two characters continually clashed in ways that made *The Odd Couple* a hit play, movie, and television series.

Many real life people find themselves in similar situations, on the job or at home, which do not seem to be nearly so funny as *The Odd Couple*. Two people can be in the same situation and have different experiences, because they pay more attention to different types of information. In a sense they speak different languages, but the languages sound so familiar that most of us overlook the differences we hear.

A person who says, "Listen to what I say," is using *hearing* language. "Look at this from my point of view" is *seeing* language. "You seem to be in touch with the way I feel" is *feeling* language. See what I mean? You can pick up on lots of these words if you listen for them.

You can avoid the *Odd Couple* type of unpleasantness by noticing which kinds of information people prefer at that time, then following their lead.

When you know what to listen for, people will often tell you how they prefer to process information. To make that processing easier for them, you can give them information the way they like it. If you were visiting Spain, it would make sense to say you can get along better and exchange information easier by speaking Spanish. But *seeing, hearing* and *feeling* languages all seem like the same language until we understand the difference.

A good rule of thumb is **use the language of the people you are dealing with.**

An expression like "I see what you're saying" may sound strange until you realize the person who says it is telling you how she processed information. She heard what you said and saw a picture of it in her head. If you then start using *seeing* words, painting verbal pictures, and put in a lot of colors, sizes, shapes and perspectives, she will have a clearer picture of what you say. She will understand you better, and she will feel that you understand her. After all, you speak the same language.

You can use the same technique to promote harmony with someone who tells you he prefers dealing with sounds. When you talk to him in *hearing* language and familiar tones, you may well hear him say, "I hear you."

To reach out and touch someone who prefers feeling information, use *feeling* language.

Becoming aware that people tend to prefer one sense for processing information at certain times has led many into another trap—labeling people and expecting them to be that way all the time. John Grinder says to be cautious, because the labels are good for just a short time, so keep checking.

Actually, many people will stay with one system for longer periods. It is a habit and they are used to it. But keep checking, because every moment brings them to a crossroads with several ways to go.

Begin to notice what people show and tell you about the systems they prefer. Practice using the languages and behaviors of the senses so you can easily send messages in any one of them. That is easier said than done, and it is easier to do than it might look. Being able to recognize the system another person is using and to communicate in that system are valuable skills.

TRAP 8
"Body Language"

One night police officer Garry Webber stopped a car for a traffic violation, and the driver opened his door to get out. As he did so, his child's toy gun fell onto the pavement. The driver bent down to pick up the toy, and Officer Webber, not able to see what the object was, drew his service revolver. Fortunately, the driver realized what he was doing and put his hands up to show they were empty.

Others have not been so fortunate. Law enforcement officers have shot people who appeared to be going for a weapon and were not. Of course people do go for weapons and shoot officers, so officers have to decide what a person's actions mean in an extremely short time.

For years researchers extensively investigated kinesics, also known as nonverbal communication. Then some popularized versions of these ideas hit the paperback shelves and magazine stands, and "body language" became a common term.

From these mass-market books some people got the idea that the positions pictured in the books always had the same meaning. Thus we find people saying, "See, her arms are crossed, so she is 'closed and rejecting,'" even though crossed arms can also indicate she is tired, cold, self-conscious or unconsciously matching someone else.

The conclusions in "body language" books came from showing various body positions to groups of people and asking what they meant. This means that "body language" is defined by the receiver, not the sender. We can get into trouble when we see a person with arms and legs crossed, say to ourselves, "Well, 73 percent of the observers said this meant "closed and rejecting," so this person is closed and rejecting." When you want to *send* a message, it is useful to know how most people are likely to interpret your actions. When you are interpreting others' actions, you need specific information about those individuals.

TRAP 8A
"The Body Can't Lie"

Writing for law enforcement officers, George J. Thompson said, "On the street when you have a choice of words or body, go with the body." In a life-or-death situation the body is much more dangerous, but those are special circumstances. I have actually heard people say, "Go with the body. *The body never lies.*" Never is a long, long time.

"Body language" hit the popular culture about the same time as "back to nature" and various "consciousness-raising" movements. Some of these people decided that "body language" is better than words, because words are deliberate, conscious and can be deceptive; whereas the body is natural, unconscious, innocent and honest. But is it?

Think of people who use their bodies to deceive others for fun or profit: magicians, basketball players, football players, card players, nervous public speakers, teachers who feel rotten but must carry on, everybody keeping a stiff upper lip, and more.

If the body never lies, there would be no acting. But many actors—in show business and in real life—convincingly portray people they aren't and feelings they don't have. If you think lying means intentional or unintentional deception, bodies do lie. Or maybe they don't. Maybe these actors believe in their roles so much that they *become* the people they are portraying and their bodies aren't lying. That might explain this line from Zig Ziglar: "The body doesn't lie, and that's just one of the reasons *you should learn to lean forward with the complete expectancy of making the sale when you ask for the order.*"

Is that sentence a contradiction or not? . Is it saying to learn to lie with your body? If you have complete expectancy when you lean forward, you won't be lying. But what if your expectancy is incomplete?

The trap is in thinking "body language" is infallible. Even if the body doesn't lie, it can fool you unless you have reliable reference clues for each person you deal with. Then you can get valuable information from nonverbal signals.

If the words and the behavior don't seem to match, you can *probably* get more accurate information from the behavior—not always. Some people have unusual behavior.

**TRAP 9
Unclear Signals**

What if your own words don't seem to match your behavior or the message you want to send? If it can happen to others, it could happen to you. And you might not ever notice—except to wonder why people react strangely to you.

Zig Ziglar says, "He can lie with his mouth; he can't lie with his body." But what if he never learned the "right" way to tell the truth with his body? What if he is in the habit of shaking his head from side to side to mean yes? He won't be lying when he shakes his head and says, "Yes," but people who see and hear him will be confused, and those who believe the body can't lie will think he's lying.

Is this far-fetched? Not very far. Similar things do happen.

Actors are aware of what their bodies do and train them to do what they want. Politicians and business executives hire image consultants to help get their acts together. These consultants evaluate their clients and train them to send clear signals.

If you can't afford a consultant, ask a good friend, use a video tape recorder or a mirror. Find out if your words and your behavior are in synch, and practice making sure they are.

Remember this about any message you send, verbal or nonverbal. The result is determined by how the other people respond. Your message is effective when you get the response you want. Most people pay little attention to the words they use or to the effects those words have on readers and listeners. And they are even less concerned with nonverbal messages, because they do not realize they are sending those signals.

John T. Molloy has done research with thousands of people in many corporations. If you want to be successful, he recommends that you dress, stand, sit, walk and talk the way successful people do. People expect someone in a certain position to behave—walk, talk, dress, even eat—in a particular way. They expect expressions, postures and other behaviors to fit in with certain accepted standard meanings. If your behaviors don't agree with their expectations, people either jump to wrong conclusions or become thoroughly confused. Neither of these responses helps you—unless you want to confuse people.

Sending unintended signals can also be hazardous to your health and safety. In her self defense programs Debbie Gardner says a potentially dangerous person will notice a person's behavior. She says muggers, rapists and others looking for victims like to see a person with "eyes locked straight ahead, shoulders slightly hunched, walking like a robot, and hardly breathing...This may be just the signal he needs to go ahead and follow through with the attack...He's looking for a victim, not a hassle."

If you look, sound, and act like a victim, you have an excellent chance of being victimized. If you look, sound, and act as if you can take care of yourself, you probably won't have to prove it. People tend to accept others as what they appear to be, until they have evidence to the contrary.

With this in mind, it makes sense to give people the kinds of nonverbal messages they expect from a person like you in that situation. Maintain eye contact, but don't stare. Keep an "open" posture. Smile when appropriate. Look angry when you're angry, and look happy when you're happy. Make it easy for others to read your signals accurately, because few people know as much about the individuality of nonverbal behavior as you do.

To help others understand easily, keep your signals clear and coordinated with each other. This may be easier said than done, because most nonverbal messages are automatic and outside our awareness. You can, however, control many of them by paying attention to the way you dress, stand, sit, walk and talk.

Another approach is to get your act together by focusing on attitudes and TARGETS—the big picture rather than pieces. If you have a clear TARGET you really want (Chapter 6), and if you have teamed up to hit the other person's TARGET (Chapter 7), and if you are in a resourceful attitude (Chapter 10), you will find it easier to send clear, coordinated messages.

TRAP 10
"But I told her in plain English."

In 1987 the Reagan Administration was embarrassed, probably because of one word. We found out that Supreme Court nominee Douglas Ginsberg had "experimented with marijuana." Ginsberg withdrew, and people wondered how the FBI investigation could miss that information. FBI Director William Sessions said Ginsberg's friends and associates had lied when asked if Ginsberg had "abused" marijuana or any other drug.

A reporter for National Public Radio asked what *abused* meant, and Sessions said one puff of a marijuana cigarette constituted abuse. Then the reporter suggested that the term might mean something else to the people at Harvard who said they weren't aware of any *abuse*. Sessions said that was a good point and the FBI should think about rephrasing the question.

When the plain English words you use have an entirely different meaning for the person who hears them, you will have a hard time getting the response you want.

What can you do about it? Be aware that words are not carved in stone, and the dictionary is not the final word. Dictionaries just report on how words have been used. They cannot tell you how the words relate to the experiences of the person you are talking to. Use words that person is most likely to understand, notice the responses you get, and find out what those responses mean. Remember your TARGET. You need to get the response you want, not to prove you selected the right word.

Notice the words others use and respond to. You can start with broad categories, then narrow them down. For example,

- Language - English, Spanish, Japanese, etc.
- Thought process language - see, hear, feel
- Technical language/jargon - medical, computer, financial, musical, psychological
  - Specific words - Navy blue, F above high C, 17 pounds
  - Pet words - awesome, mutual trust, ON TARGET.

That list is similar to the one in Chapter 11 for building mutual trust. Trust and understanding are closely related. We tend to trust people we understand and who, we think, understand us. So when we speak Spanish to a Costa Rican, we are likely to develop more trust and understanding than if we spoke Urdu.

Use the same *thought process languages* (see, feel or hear) your listeners use to make it easier for them to process the information. Otherwise they may have to translate your message—for example, from seeing language into feeling language. You can see that they might have a rough time getting a handle on your ideas. By paying attention to words and eye movements, such as those on the Show and Tell Chart on page 124, you can figure out which kinds of words to use. With a little practice, you can become fluent in seeing, hearing and feeling languages.

For people who share a *technical language or jargon*, word choice can be somewhat easier. These languages have precise terms for certain objects and processes. A few words can carry a lot of information—to people who know the language. They also carry another kind of message to people who do not know the language, and that message can trigger confusion or resentment.

Specific words can help you avoid misunderstandings. *Navy blue* is more specific than *a dark color*. *F above high C* is more specific than *a high note*. *Seventeen pounds* is more specific than *heavy*. Mothers tell small children, "Clean up your room," then get angry when the rooms are not as neat as they would have made them. The closer you get to what you will see, hear, or feel, the less room there is for misunderstanding.

Pet words and phrases. When you have a choice of words, you will enhance understanding if you choose a word or phrase the other person likes to use. Other words might be just as good for you, but not have the same meaning for that person. Since words don't mean exactly the same to others as they do to you, you might as well use words they are comfortable with. If they like *awesome,* use *awesome* rather than *phenomenal* or *splendid.*

Notice the responses you get. If those responses indicate your words are not understood or were not effective, use other words or other ways to send your message.

But What Does it Mean?

Right now we are using a language in which a *fat chance* and a *slim chance* are the same thing. It seems remarkable that we can communicate with words at all. It is even more remarkable that we actually do quite well at it in most situations, so it is easy to fall into the trap of taking words and their meanings for granted. We assume that everyone understands a word the same way we do. We get the job done, so it doesn't seem to matter.

When it does matter, you can choose to let people form their own conclusions, or you can use words which are more likely to get them to come closer to what you have in mind.

Stan Parker once made a talk in which he said "musical instrument" several times without mentioning a specific instrument. In the discussion afterward three people referred to that musical instrument. One called it a violin, one called it a guitar and one said flute.

Since we cannot have a picture, mental or otherwise, of a "musical instrument," those who like to process information visually will select a representative instrument to picture. That is what these people did. They heard "musical instrument," made a mental image of a specific instrument and stored it. When they remembered it later, they saw those images and described what they saw—a violin, a guitar and a flute. People who think like this often say "I see what you're saying."

If the type of instrument had been important to his talk, Stan could have said "Steinway concert grand piano". It wasn't, so he let his listeners make up their own minds.

In a *Saturday Night Live* sketch Ed Asner played a man retiring from a nuclear power plant in California. At a going-away party he told the other workers, "Remember, you can't put too much water in a nuclear reactor."

After he left the others began to wonder whether he meant it is impossible to put too much water in a nuclear reactor, or they need not worry because no amount of water can harm a nuclear reactor, or it is dangerous to put too much water in a nuclear reactor. They decided he meant not to worry.

The scene shifted to Asner on a beach in Hawaii with his girl friend. She said, "Oh, look at that bright light!" He said, "A nuclear power plant must have blown up. You know, you can't look too long at a nuclear explosion."

Many of us tend to wander through life seeing and hearing words and presuming we understand the message. We also spend a lot of time doing things over after misunderstanding the first time—sometimes even the second and third.

How can we prevent that kind of misunderstanding and get things right the first time? By asking the right questions.

If someone calls and says, "I'm coming to visit, will you meet my plane?" you need to know

> What airline?
> What flight? From where?
> When is it scheduled to arrive?
> Which airport?

If you send a note announcing a visit, you must include all that information, if you want the receiver to meet your plane. Ask yourself those questions to make sure you cover all bases.

Do you remember this one? "I'll hold this stake, and when I nod my head, you hit it with that hammer." That's cute in a Laurel and Hardy movie, but we want to prevent such comic—and tragic—situations in your life by getting it right the first time.

When the sales manager says, "Send the Amalgamated order next-day air," the shipping manager can handle it as long as there is only one Amalgamated order and they use only one overnight carrier. Otherwise, the shipping manager must ask, "Which Amalgamated order? Which carrier?" But the sales manager can head off any possible confusion by anticipating and answering those questions before sending the message.

Remember Murphy's Law. *Anything that can go wrong will.*

John Grinder and Richard Bandler identified a number of word use patterns which can confuse or mislead, and they developed a systematic way to go about getting specific needed information from people using these patterns. They say the most accurate information is that which is closest to an actual experience. When you use words, make them specific see, hear and feel words. They are easiest to interpret accurately.

When FBI agents asked about *abusing* marijuana, they asked people to make a judgement based on their interpretation of the word. If they ask about *smoking* marijuana, they might get a different answer.

To get it right the first time, notice whether you, or those you are communicating with, have all the information needed. If not, start asking appropriate questions. What? Where? When? Who? How? All? None? Compared to what? What will happen if I do?

Keep asking until you have a clear picture, sound, and feeling to act on.

TRAP 11
"But it worked before."

When something works, we tend to repeat it. By the time we do it enough times to discover that it does not work every time, it is already a habit or a superstition. Then we ignore it. If it works often enough to be useful, we keep doing it and never find out whether something else works better.

Here's how we form superstitions. Ted Nettles wins a tennis tournament, so the next time he goes to a tournament, he wears exactly the same clothes, eats exactly the same breakfast, leaves at exactly the same time, and warms up exactly the same way with the same racquet. Very little in that routine can influence the outcome of a tournament, *except* as it affects Ted's mind. If going through this ritual triggers the same attitude he had when he won the other tournament, it can help. Yet he can get the same effect much easier by remembering how he felt while he was winning. The routine is superstitious because Ted did not test it to find out which, if any, of its pieces actually affected his play in the tournament.

If Ted were to go so far as to also play tennis exactly the same way he did before, he will be in trouble. As soon as his opponents recognize his routine, they will take advantage of it, and Ted will lose his matches.

Through superstition, habit or both we tend to repeat the same patterns. We find that sometimes they work better than they do at other times, and sometimes they do not work at all.

We fall into this trap when we expect certain words or actions to work on everybody, every time or in every situation. When we have that much faith in a routine, we quit noticing whether or not it is appropriate. In fact, we do not notice much except, perhaps, that we don't get results we want very often. Then we wonder what is wrong with the other people.

Avoid falling in love with one routine, one set of words or actions. You'll find more on this when you get to Chapter 13. Be aware that people and circumstances vary. Notice what works and what does not work, and select your verbal and nonverbal messages accordingly.

TRAP 12
"What else could I do?"

At a high school assembly a group of the school's finest musicians played one of the popular songs of the day. The audience's applause demanded an encore, and after some hesitation and deliberation, the group played an encore. They played the same song, because that is the only one they had rehearsed.

Sometimes necessity limits our choices, but often we limit those choices by our own habits. The more choices we have to in any situation, the more likely we are to succeed. Any one of those musicians could have played several solo selections, but together they could play just one song, so they were limited to situations which did not require more than one song.

The Boston Pops Orchestra has many selections in its library and plenty of time to rehearse, so the Boston Pops can play several concerts in a season, complete with encores.

As Chapter 13 points out, effective communicators choose from a variety of responses. The more choices you have, the more situations you can deal with effectively.

TRAP 13
"You just can't get along with some people."

Executive Ella Reeder had come to New York for a 15-minute appointment with financier Joshua Barrington to discuss a deal which would be beneficial to her company. She had talked with Barrington twice before, briefly, and found him to be "one of those people you just can't get through to." This time, however, Ella noticed Barrington say,"I feel..." so she began to throw in every *feeling* word she could think of. In a few minutes it seemed as though Barrington ("Call me Josh.") was her best friend. Ella's 15-minute appointment lasted more than two hours, and Josh Barrington's advice did benefit her company.

Most of us get along well with some people, and not at all with others. We usually have some traits in common with the ones we get along with. The others rub us the wrong way, or vice versa. We don't see eye-to-eye, we cannot talk to them, etc. It would be nice if we could avoid people like that. Unfortunately they often turn up as employers, employees, teachers, students, landlords, tenants, relatives, and others we have to deal with from time to time.

Believing we cannot get along with certain people is a trap which prevents us from doing things which can prime the communication pump, so in certain circumstances this belief limits our ability to get to our TARGET. You can avoid this trap when you realize you have more choices than you thought you had, and you have the tools to improve those conditions.

However, to hit your TARGET, you must take responsibility for building the necessary level of mutual trust and comfort. You will find several ways to do this described in Chapter 11. Your first step is to adjust your attitude and your perspective. When you put yourself in the other person's position, you can understand how he can do those things which annoy you. Then get on his side, speak his language, build some trust (starting with yourself) and notice how the situation improves.

Psychologist Nancy Henley says people "adopt mirror-image reflections of each other when they are in harmony; or show great discoordination when they disagree." They are synchronized in "such postures as legs crossed in the same manner, similar standing positions, hand to chin or hip, or arms similarly folded."

Some of this happens so fast we do not notice, all of it is habit, an automatic response cued by a harmonious atmosphere. So when we match other people's postures, gestures, voices, or breathing, we are sending them the subtle message that they are in a harmonious atmosphere.

You have a lot of tools for getting results you want by effective communicating. Many of those tools can help you deal with people who rub you the wrong way and vice versa, so you can avoid the "just can't get along with them" trap. People you "can't get along with" have no reason to come over to your side. But as a knowledgeable communicator, you can expand your boundaries to get on their side.

> **TRAP 14**
> "Those _____ are all alike."

Adventure comes to a home when a little tyke gets into the canned goods and removes all the labels. Labels on cans, bottles, boxes, and bags give us a reliable indication of what is inside. We can be pretty sure a can labeled "Beans" will have beans in it, no matter when or where we open it.

When we carry that confidence over to the labels we put on people, however, we could be headed for a trap. Labels are words we use to classify people when we lump them into groups so we do not have to deal with them individually. Here are some labels we might find in our mass media.

Conservative	Liberal	Moderate
Consumer	Adult	Voter
Motorist	Pedestrian	Businessman
Parent	Adolescent	Taxpayer

Those are words which describe things people do or think. Some of them are adjectives used as nouns. We decide what labels to use by selecting one or more qualities which fit a particular classification and ignore everything else. We judge the whole person—this complex human being—by a couple of characteristics. If we have any further dealings with that person, though, we may be surprised to find the label did not stick—if we pay attention. Actually, all the labels listed can apply to one person, but not at the same time.

Classifying or labeling is a quick, easy way to deal with the deluge of information coming our way. First impressions often become permanent labels. And labels can take the place of accurate information. Alfred Korzybski said a person is a process, not a fixed object, and any person has more characteristics than any label can account for.

Ronald Reagan is a Democrat. That label is accurate—if we are in the 1950's or before. But that label is out of date in the 1980's. Labels have a way of doing that. Whenever you see or hear a label applied to anybody, by yourself or by someone else, ask "When? Does this label still apply?"

Be alert for any statement like "This person is a _____." That _____ is a label, and things with labels can be mislabeled, and labels can be misleading.

Traps Review

One way to succeed is to avoid shooting yourself in the foot. People tend to shoot themselves in the foot repeatedly by doing things they think they should do. To avoid this, learn to recognize and avoid the communication traps we continually fall into.

Expecting others to behave as we expect them to, ignoring signals, and misinterpreting clues can lead us into these traps.

TRAP 1: Expecting anyone to act as someone else does
TRAP 2: Paying attention to our intentions rather than others' responses
TRAP 3: Arguing to change someone's mind
TRAP 3A: Thinking there are only two sides to any question
TRAP 4: Overlooking others' contrary reactions
TRAP 4A: Overlooking our own contrary reactions
TRAP 5: Misinterpreting eye contact
TRAP 6: Expecting others to want change, or sameness, without checking
TRAP 7: Ignoring the ways others process information
TRAP 8: Trusting "body language" without individual references
TRAP 9: Sending mixed messages
TRAP 10: Expecting others to interpret words the same way we do
TRAP 11: Expecting one approach to work all the time
TRAP 12: Thinking we have only one way to do something
TRAP 13: Thinking we can't get along with some people
TRAP 14: Labeling

> He had the calm confidence of
> a Christian with four aces.
> *Mark Twain*

> No one can make you feel inferior
> without your consent.
> *Eleanor Roosevelt*

10

ESTABLISH RESOURCEFUL ATTITUDES

Dumbo, the little elephant in the movie of the same name, could fly by flapping his extra-large ears, but Dumbo didn't believe he could fly until his friend Timothy the mouse gave him a "magic" feather. With the feather Dumbo could fly like a... well, he could fly. Without the feather he couldn't—until Timothy convinced him that the ability to fly was in his mind, and ears. Then Dumbo flew like a flying elephant.

Dumbo could fly, but only when he *thought* he could. That happens to a lot of us—not flying by flapping our ears, but taking on self-defeating attitudes which prevent us from soaring in our own unique ways. When we look closely at the pressure situations we find ourselves in, we find that most of the pressure is self-inflicted.

If you follow the results of the pro golf tour, you may have noticed that the tournament leaders on Thursday and Friday are often relatively unknown, players who have not won much. When a tournament is over on Sunday, however, the leader is usually someone experienced at winning golf tournaments.

The early-round leaders use the same balls and clubs on Saturday and Sunday as on Thursday and Friday. They play on the same course, and they still have the ability to play golf. Nothing else can affect a player's score—except attitude.

Nobody notices an unknown player, but a tournament leader attracts attention which leads to thoughts like, "If I'm not careful, I'll blow it." The key words are "I'll blow it." That is self-inflicted pressure and self-fulfilling prophecy.

People with an I-can't-do-it attitude have little chance of succeeding. They get distracted thinking about not being able to do it. They feel rotten, and they probably blow it.

With a confident, resourceful attitude they have a good chance of succeeding at anything they have the ability to do. They can relax and concentrate. Their thoughts, if any, are on what they are doing, not whether they can do it. They feel good, and they can handle the situation.

Though few people feel calm, confident, and competent in all situations, almost everybody alive is confident about something. We have all had experiences we can use as resources.

This may be news to some people, especially those who find it easier to recall negative events and feelings than positive ones. Some blame this on a poor self-image, but where does that come from. Think about this. The events we are most likely to remember are the ones associated with a strong emotional response. The negative emotions attached to our experiences tend to be much stronger than the positive ones. This is especially true for experiences in childhood when we formed our attitudes about many things. We were not prepared to protect ourselves, and we could not put things in the proper perspective.

Positive and *negative, good* and *bad, pleasant* and *unpleasant,* by the way, are words we use to describe our emotional responses to experiences. An experience is an event like the close play at the plate in the baseball game several years ago. Umpire Bill Klem didn't say anything, and the catcher asked if the runner was safe or out. Klem said, "He's nothing until I call it."

When we have strong feelings about an experience, we usually label *the experience* positive or devastating or whatever we feel is appropriate. Later, when we think of a similar experience, we stick the same label on it. Those labels influence our attitudes about certain types of events.

Aiming at a certain TARGET, you may face a situation labeled "negative," even though you may have improved your skills since the time you applied that label—a time you may have lacked confidence, pressured yourself, or attempted more than you could handle. Whatever brought it on, the negative label on that experience doesn't help you.

You may also find your mind occupied with other matters so you just ignore your attitude. That won't help you either.

Before you start communicating with people who can help you hit your TARGET, it is a good idea make sure you feel confident, resourceful and anything else you need to be at your best. This lets you concentrate on what you are doing rather than on some imagined inadequacies.

It is also a good idea to make sure people you deal with are attentive and receptive. If they are not, you may as well be somewhere else doing something productive.

You can establish resourceful attitudes with one or more of these methods.

- Recall resourceful attitudes from your past.
- Take on physical aspects of the attitude you need.
- Rehearse mentally.
- Prepare and rehearse until you know you can only be brilliant at what you are going to do.

ATTITUDES FROM YOUR PAST

Donna Elder discovered, to her chagrin, that serving on the church stewardship committee required her to visit several church members—some of whom she barely knew—and ask them to pledge money for next year's budget. Donna tended to be shy around people she didn't know very well, and she didn't like to ask people for money. With a nobody-likes-this-but-we-have-to-do-it-so-let's-get-it-over-with attitude, Donna has dim prospects for this project.

But those prospects brightened considerably when Donna adopted an attitude associated with another kind of experience. Vivacious and charming around people she knows well, Donna went back in her memory to a time when she was particularly outgoing. Remembering what she saw, what she heard and what she felt at the time, Donna got back into the same frame of mind. She wanted that attitude when she made her visits, so she practiced until she could bring it back any time she wanted.

Then Donna had another problem. She enjoyed the visits so much she had to force herself to keep them short enough so she could get them all in.

The process Donna went through is a simplified version of what a "method" actor goes through to prepare for a role on stage or screen. If a role calls for tenderness, the actor recalls a time when he was tender. If a role calls for suffering, the actor recalls a time when she was suffering. If a role calls for joy, the actor recalls a joyful time.

The feelings or attitudes we've had are still stored in our memories, and we can use them whenever we want to. Can you remember a special moment when everything went your way, when you succeeded far beyond your expectations? Do you recall how you felt at that moment?

Can you think of other situations in which you would like to feel that same way and succeed to the same degree? That experience is stored and available at a moment's notice. If you can remember the details of an event—what you saw, heard and felt—your attitude at that time will also return.

Attitude Adjustment Experiment #1

A. Think of a specific time when you did something so well and so easily that it surprised you. As you think of that event, mentally
   See what you saw,
   Hear what you heard,
   Feel what you felt.
Notice how you feel as you re-experience the event. Notice the changes in your breathing, posture, relaxation, etc.

B. Repeat the process and, as those feelings reach their peak intensity, take a deep breath, squeeze your left wrist.

C. Think of something else for a moment, then take a deep breath and squeeze your wrist.

D. Practice A, B, and C until you automatically get the feelings associated with your successful experience whenever you take a deep breath or squeeze your wrist.

PHYSICAL ASPECTS

Darrell Teller had America's number one fear, performance anxiety. It used to be stage fright, but it got a new name. Darrell hated to speak in front of large groups of people—five or more. He knew his subject, he could put words together, he could speak intelligible sentences, and his career would benefit if he would make speeches. But when Darrell thought of standing in front of several people and of all that could go wrong, his throat got dry and his stomach seemed to be tied in knots.

Then Darrell found out confidence is a matter of attitude, and he went after better attitudes. He noticed how confident attitudes look and sound. He found that confident speakers stand straight, hold their heads up, look people in the eye, move decisively, and talk with a full voice. And they breathe.

Darrell also remembered, vividly, that on the few occasions he had attempted a speech his shoulders slumped, his head was down, his eyes looked down, he wondered what to do with his hands, his voice was thin and tended to get caught in his throat, and he breathed as little as possible.

With practice Darrell closed the gap. He can look and sound like a confident person. And he can do it when he wants to. If he notices a symptom of unconfident Darrell, he automatically snaps back into his confident attitude. But that doesn't happen very much. It turns out that when he began acting confidently, he began to feel confident, and he could turn his attention to his audience where it belonged.

A "technical" actor observes the ways people display various emotions or attitudes, then reproduces or adapts these outward signs to portray a character.

According to William James, the "father of American psychology," when we feel an emotion, we show the physical signs of that emotion; and when we show the physical signs of an emotion, we begin to feel that emotion. Outward appearance is a reflection of inner attitude and vice versa.

If that really happens, then Donna Deacon will look and sound confident and vivacious when visiting, and Darrell Teller will feel more confident when breathing and standing straight.

Well, it does happen. If it didn't, the "method" would'nt work. Actor's don't intend to feel a certain way, but to convince audiences they do. The only way audiences can tell is by seeing what actors do, and hearing what they say, and how they say it.

Attitude Adjustment Experiment #2

A. Stand or sit with your head down, shoulders slumped, cheeks and jaw slack, and breathing as little as possible. Notice how you feel in that position.

B. Now take a deep breath, stand or sit erect, pull your shoulders back, put some life into your face, and continue to breathe deeply. Notice how you feel in that position, and compare it with the way you felt in position A.

C. Now smile and compare the way you feel with the way you felt in positions A and B.

MENTAL REHEARSAL

In February of 1982 I decided to take part in a program which included going through a ropes course, which consisted of walking on wires stretched various distances from the ground and climbing things. People who had been through similar courses described the feature event, standing on a one-foot-wide platform on top of a 30-foot-high pole and leaping to catch a metal ring hanging several feet away.

Even though I would wear a safety harness and everything was safe, I was nervous about the idea of standing on top of a 30-foot swaying pole. The program was in September, so I had almost six months to think about it.

Well, during that six months I stood on that pole hundreds of times in my mind. I saw what it was like from up there, I saw the ring, and I felt myself jumping for it.

By the time I got to the top of the real pole, I had no thoughts of danger. In fact, I had been there so many times that it was old stuff. I was almost disappointed.

The process called *visualization* came up in Chapter 6 as it relates to testing TARGETS. Another use for it is in mental rehearsal and establishing attitudes.

Maxwell Maltz cited several examples of people using "mental pictures." to improve attitudes and skills. They include shooting free throws, playing piano, interviewing for jobs, and improving self-image. Maltz wrote,

> You want your mental pictures to approximate actual experience as much as possible. The way to do this is pay attention to small details, sights, sounds, objects, in your imagined environment. One of my patients was using this exercise to overcome her fear of the dentist. She was unsuccessful, until she began to notice small details in her imagined picture—the smell of the antiseptic in the office, the feel of the leather on the chair arms, the sight of the dentist's well-manicured nails as his hands approached her mouth, etc.

Notice that these mental "pictures" include sights, sounds, smells and feelings.

John Grinder says, when you rehearse mentally, "You never have to do anything the first time." Emerson said, "The greater part of courage is in having done the thing before." Those are two benefits of mental rehearsal.

> **Attitude Adjustment Experiment #3**
> A. Think of an event you will be involved in soon. Pick something which is not routine.
> B. Mentally go through the process step by step, and make sure it turns out the way you want it to. (It's also a good idea to do all the preparation you would normally do.)
> C. Continue to mentally rehearse until the event takes place.
> D. When the event is over, review it and notice what your attitude was like.

PREPARATION/REHEARSAL

Danny Manning was on the free throw line. The basketball game was on the line. The national championship was on the line. Manning's Kansas team was ahead by two points with five seconds left to play. If he made two free throws, his team would be assured of winning the championship. If he didn't, the high-scoring Oklahoma team had a good chance to win.

Shooting free throws involves rhythm, timing, form and habit. These all come from practice. The more people practice making free throws, the more confident they become, and the more confident they are, the more free throws they make. The big test is under pressure in a big game. Putting the ball through the hoop is automatic—if the shooter has the right attitude.

With years of experience, Danny Manning knew he could make two free throws, so he could relax and let his well-trained muscles take over. He made the free throws to win the game.

Once it got off the ground, America's manned space program had a string of impressive achievements. Their actual execution, however, seemed almost routine. But everyone involved in the space flights had rehearsed the procedures so many times that the people not only had developed the necessary skills, they also had confidence based on experience.

Succeeding at something increases our confidence that we can do it again. So one way to establish a resourceful attitude is to rehearse what you intend to do until you are letter-perfect.

A carpenter can drive his thousandth nail much straighter and faster than he did his first. His brain has a routine system of signals to his muscles, which are accustomed to the nail-driving procedure. By the time he has driven 10,000 nails, he has the attitude that he can pretty much handle any nail-driving situation.

You probably don't think much about it, but I'd guess you have that same attitude toward washing your hands, tying your shoes, and things like that. Why not? You've done them enough.

You can rehearse the same way to play in a piano recital, give a talk before a group, or any other activity.

Attitude Adjustment Experiment #4

A. Practice. Do whatever you're going to do until it is second nature to you.
B. Do it.
C. Review and notice your attitude.

OTHERS' ATTITUDES

You also need to make sure the others involved with your TARGETS are in resourceful, attentive attitudes. If they are not, you might as well be somewhere else doing something productive. How can you tell? Be alert for any of these signs.

- Shoulders slumped
- Head down
- Shallow breathing
- Thin voice
- Lack of response

These signs have come up before in this chapter. They are fairly reliable indicators of a less-than-desirable state. They usually show up when people are focused on something going on inside their heads and the outside world is tuned out.

Before you can accomplish much with people in this state, you need to get their attention, then get them into a more resourceful attitude. What gets their attention? Sights, sounds and feelings. You can do something to attract their eyes, make a sound to catch their ears, or touch them somehow.

Once you have their attention, you can establish another attitude by asking about something they are interested in or an especially pleasant experience. Thinking about such things also bring back the pleasant feelings which go with them. Thinking about something interesting gets a person interested.

Another way to get someone more alert is to get him to shift his posture or breathing. If you want to be subtle, ask about something on a top shelf or on the ceiling. That should get him to look at the spot you mentioned, and looking up will bring his head up. Do anything to get him into a more alert position, paying attention, and breathing.

You might find yourself with a person who is alert and attentive to things outside herself, but not to you. Some people talk on the phone, converse with others, sign papers, and carry on as if you weren't there. Remember, eye contact is not necessary for attention, but some kind of responsiveness is. Either do something to get it or leave. In fact, leaving can be one way to do it. "Excuse me. I see you are busy with other things. Perhaps I could come back when it is more convenient."

Hank Tisler said, "If the customer isn't listening, why talk?"

Attitude Review

With a resourceful attitude you are confident. You concentrate on what you are doing rather than how you are feeling or what you are thinking. This attitude is the foundation for communicating to hit a TARGET. You can establish a resourceful attitude in one of these ways.

- Retrieve resourceful attitudes by thinking of a specific time when you had that attitude. Practice until you can instantly bring back the feelings associated with that event.
- Establish a resourceful attitude by taking on the outward aspects of that attitude—erect posture, head up, eye contact, regular deep breathing, and full voice.
- Build confidence by rehearsing mentally.
- Practice until you are sure you can do what you want to do.

Others involved must also have resourceful or attentive attitudes, or you may be wasting your time.

- Notice posture, breathing, voice quality and response.
- If the signs do not indicate a desirable attitude, get their attention, then get them into a more responsive state.
   - Get them to move into a more alert position, or
   - Ask about a something which will produce the desired attitude.

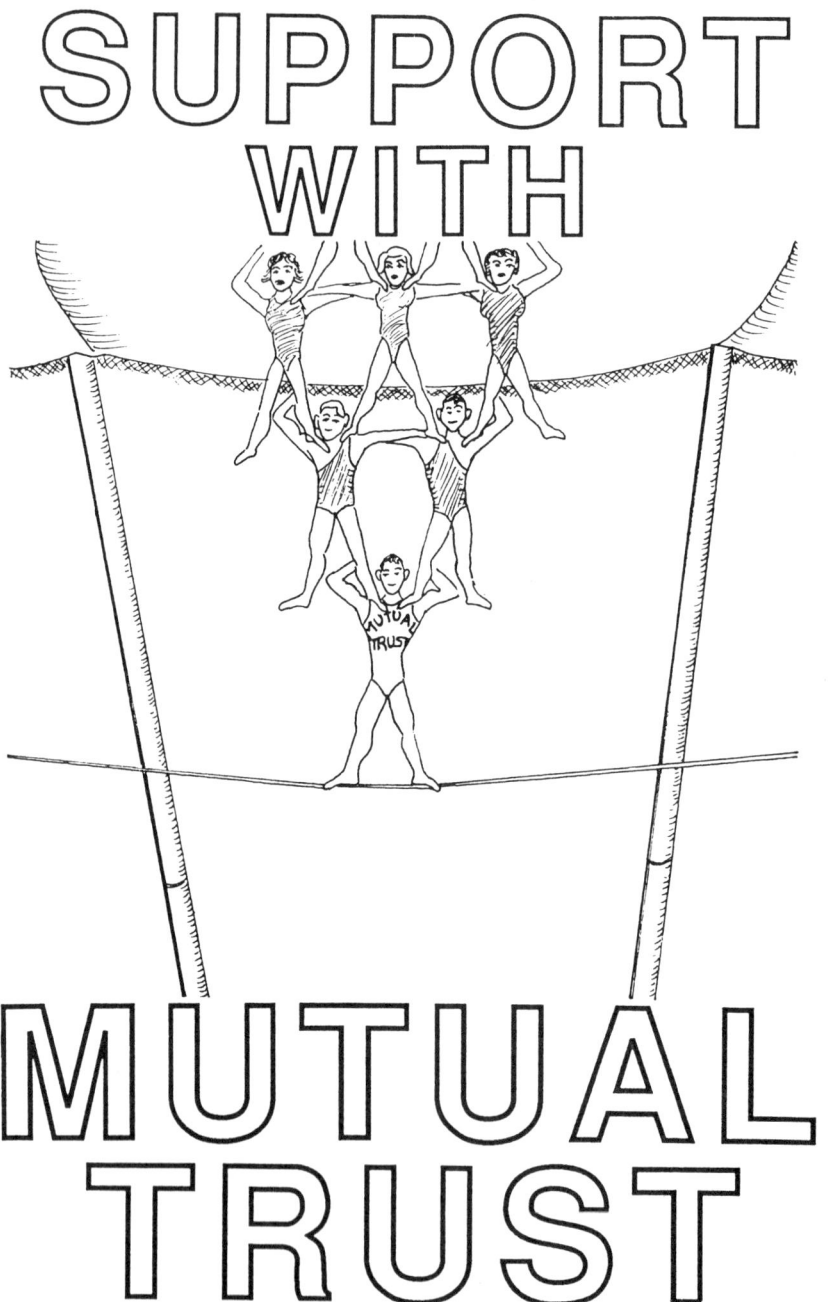

> People need assurances that others
> are just like themselves.
> *Karl Menninger*

> Did you ever get the feeling that
> the whole world's a tuxedo, and
> you're a pair of brown shoes?
> *George Gobel*

11

SUPPORT WITH MUTUAL TRUST

David Brady was in trouble. Alone at night on a Mexican street, he found himself in the path of a mob which was obviously in an anti-Gringo mood. They were turning over cars and shouting "Viva! Viva!" David, who is obviously Anglo, quickly realized the mob would catch him if he tried to run; it would get him if he stayed where he was; he could not defend himself against so many; and there was no place to hide. Meanwhile, here they came, shaking their fists in the air and shouting, "Viva! Viva!"

As the mob approached him, David fell in with the leaders, shook his fist in the air and shouted, "Viva! Viva!" He joined them for a few blocks, turned over some cars, and slipped away when he got a chance.

There is nothing like an hostile mob to test a person's communicating skill. By moving like they moved and sounding like they sounded, David gained the mob's trust enough to avoid trouble. The similarity of his actions and the mob's overrode their obvious differences.

People are more likely to respond positively to people they trust; they tend to trust people they feel comfortable around; and they feel most comfortable around people who are like themselves. How do they know others are like themselves? By what they see, hear or feel.

When we hear people speaking strange languages or wearing unusual clothes, most of us feel uncomfortable and perhaps a little apprehensive. When we can understand the language and see familiar behavior, we get more comfortable.

When people are trusting and comfortable with each other, barriers come down and interesting things happen. They begin to stand, sit, move or sound like each other. Watch people sitting together in a restaurant. Without hearing a word you can tell which ones are getting along well and which ones are not. The ones who are getting along might sit in similar positions, and they may even lift their forks or glasses at the same time. You will also notice that nobody else in the restaurant notices this is going on. It is natural. It happens all the time.

And when it happens, the people involved see and hear it. Usually it does not register with them consciously, but in the backs of their minds they notice the similarities and feel comfortable with each other.

When it does not happen, they feel uncomfortable and barriers go up. One of the most useful things a communicator can do is keep, or bring, those barriers down so trust and understanding can grow. This is too important to take chances with, so you would be wise to make trust a top priority—mutual trust, that is. And you can begin with yourself.

Trust Them

Do you trust the other person to do what you want done? If you qualified that person as recommended in Chapter 7, you probably do. If you don't trust this person to carry out an agreement, figure out what it would take for you to do so. You must be able to trust this person—at least within the limits of your TARGET.

When you order a meal in a restaurant, you trust the people to prepare and serve what you ordered, to charge you the amount stated on the menu, and to look out for your health and safety. In some cases you even trust them with your credit card and automobile. But to eat a meal, you don't have to trust them with your bank accounts, trade secrets, or innermost thoughts. You only need a trust level appropriate for the transaction.

Mutual trust starts with you, so make sure you trust the others involved. Then check their trust in you. Sometimes you can feel tension and distrust in the air. You can tell when people are talking, standing, or moving the way you are, and you can tell when they aren't. If your radar is turned on, you know whether you are getting positive responses or not.

When you have a satisfactory level of mutual trust and comfort, you don't need the rest of this chapter. But if you don't have that comfort, you will find this information useful.

Some of the steps in this book involve similar processes, and they can overlap in many cases. The Crawford Consideration discussed in Chapter 7 is an effective way to build trust and establish resourceful attitudes at the same time. And most of the steps, including this one, involve nonverbal signals.

If you feel the need to build a higher level of trust, you can use one or more of the following until you have the conditions you need for reaching your TARGET.

- Speak their language.
- Listen to them.
- Look the part.
- Match the signals:
  Voice expressions
  Posture
  Movements
  Breathing
  Pet words and phrases.
- Get on their side.

SPEAK THEIR LANGUAGE

Lee Iacocca wrote, "It's important to talk to people in their own language. If you do it well, they'll say, 'God, he said exactly what I was thinking.' And when they begin to respect you, they'll follow you to the death. The *reason* they're following you is not because you're providing some mysterious leadership. It's because you're following them."

We speak many kinds of languages—professional languages, street languages, computer languages, dialects, accents. We "speak" both verbal and nonverbal languages. These languages can enhance our communicating, and if we are not careful, they can set up barriers to both trust and understanding.

One language which gets little attention, although it has proven to be valuable tools for building mutual trust, is the language of the senses—seeing, hearing and feeling languages which often reflect the way a person is processing information.

"I see." "I hear you." "I catch on." There are three ways of saying the same thing, and each one describes a different way of understanding a message.

Bandler and Grinder and other investigators found that people tell how they are processing information with the words they breathe and move their eyes. The Show and Tell (p. 124) Chart gives you clues to determine which sensory language to use.

By using terms which correspond to the way another person is processing information, you can avoid the "We don't see eye-to-eye" trap (Chapter 9) and go a long way toward building trust and understanding.

This may seem trivial, but I have heard too many reports of people breaking the ice by matching someone's see, hear or feel language to ignore the idea. Test it yourself. Notice which of these words others use and use them yourself.

Jargon

Can you decipher or identify the languages in the following three sentences?

1. "Three equations in three unknowns can be solved by the method of elimination, as well as by the method of determinants."

2. "On the overrunning-clutch type of cranking motor, the clearance between the pinion and the thrust washer or housing should be measured with the pinion in the cranking position after assembly is completed."

3. "A comparison of the hysteresis curves of the new tape with that of two older tapes shows marked differences in their characteristics, particularly in their remanence values."

These sentences come from books on 1. algebra, 2. automobile mechanics, and 3. electronics.

Psychologists, computer people and most others in specialized areas tend to use a lot of words which mean nothing to outsiders. Unfortunately, that does not prevent many of them from using those words on outsiders. Jargon is a two-edged sword. It carries precise information to those on the inside, so if you speak the jargon, use it with those who understand. That makes you an insider.

You do yourself and your listeners a large favor when you avoid using jargon or "in-crowd" slang with people who do not understand it. How can you communicate with those people? In plain, simple English, Spanish, Japanese, or whatever language you are using.

LISTEN TO THEM

Hank Tisler wrote,

> I know of no finer way of gaining people's affections than to listen to them talk about what interests them most: themselves.

Under most circumstances, that's good advice. But be alert. If you detect signs that a person is uncomfortable, sad, or angry about a topic, change the subject. Don't pursue it.

You can get people talking about themselves by asking open-ended questions. What? Where? When? Who? How?

Almost everybody is keenly interested in something. If you can discover what a person's favorite subject is and get her talking about it, you can go a long way toward building trust and understanding—maybe even affection.

LOOK THE PART

One cause of the "generation gap" of the 1960's was the "weird" appearance of young people. They wore long hair, beards, old clothes, jeans and generally looked different from what older people were used to. From "Why don't you get a haircut?" to "As long as you live in my house you will dress decently at the dinner table," people found it hard to accept this new style.

The young folks were just "doing my own thing, man," and could not understand why they got so much abuse for expressing their individuality by adopting the current styles. The result was that the generations "could not communicate."

Then a lot of hippies and others turned into Yuppies and read *Dress for Success*. Males and females started wearing three-piece pinstripe suits to look successful. Uniforms—military, sports, school or business—help bring people together and to separate them from outsiders.

A newspaper headline read, "Man wearing necktie holds up bank." This rates a headline because it is unusual. We do not expect bank robbers to dress like that, and we do not expect people wearing ties to act that way.

Unless you enjoy overcoming handicaps, wear clothing and hair styles people expect from a person in your circumstances.

Remember, your purpose it to hit your TARGET. Unless your TARGET is to "make a fashion statement," you will probably be better off dressing in a way that makes a good impression and avoids suspicion, distrust and dislike.

SHOW AND TELL

The clues on this chart can show or tell how *a person is processing information at the time.* **CAUTION:** *These signals apply to most people, but there are exceptions. Be alert for patterns and for confirming evidence. With reliable clues you can increase trust and understanding.*

SEE	HEAR	FEEL
Eyes: looking up or straight ahead and defocused. 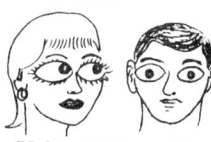	*Eyes:* looking to the side or down and left 	*Eyes:* looking down and right 
Voice: high, rapid	*Voice:* moderate pitch, volume, and rate	*Voice:* low, slow, pauses
Breathing: rapid, high, shallow 	*Breathing:* moderate rate, middle 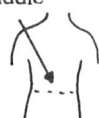	*Breathing:* slow, low, deep
Words: dawn depict flash focus gaze gleam glimpse glisten glow green look magnify peek picture red reflect see shine show sight view vision visualize watch	*Words:* amplify audible audio chime chorus hear hush listen loud melodious music noise phone recall ring say silent sing sound speak talk tell voice whisper	*Words:* angry arouse catch cold fall feel grab grasp handle happy hard heavy hit hold impress inspire pleasant push rough run smooth struggle tender touch

MATCH THE SIGNS

When people are comfortable and trust each other, they display certain outward signs. They take on each other's posture, movements or voice expressions. If one moves, the other may soon follow. In fact, some people feel uncomfortable when they are not in a position like that of the person they are talking with.

Notice how often you find people in a conversation with their arms or legs crossed or uncrossed, hands on hips, hands on chins, chins on hands, and other distinct positions. What happens when one shifts?

When you can shift one of the features discussed below and another person follows your lead, you have reached a fairly high degree of trust and comfort with that person.

One way to reach the level of mutual trust you need is to match one or more of these outward signs. If you read Chapter 8, you will be familiar with these signs.

Many of them are the same, although here we are using them for building trust rather than detecting clues.

Voice Expressions

Voices have these characteristics we can match to build trust.

> Rate of speech—fast, slow or moderate
> Volume—loud, soft or in between
> Pitch—high, low or medium
> Inflections—from monotone to much variation

Rate. Southerners tend to talk slower than Easterners. People tend to follow regional speech patterns, because that's what they are used to hearing.

People processing seeing information tend to talk faster than people dealing with feeling information. Some individuals speak slowly and others talk rapidly. Many are somewhere in between. A person's rate of speech can vary with the situation and the mood, so be alert for the current rates and match them.

People who speak rapidly often complain that they get impatient listening to a slow talker. People who speak slowly often complain that they cannot understand a fast talker. (Think about that term.) If you notice a difference between your rate of speech and that of someone else, you can make that person more comfortable by adjusting your rate accordingly.

Volume. Some people are loud and some speak softly. When one person is much louder than another, one can be uncomfortable. Maybe both. One might say, "He's a loudmouth," and the other might say, "Why doesn't she speak up? The loud speaker might have impaired hearing and would appreciate others' speaking louder so he can hear. And he might not. Most people do not realize how they sound to others, so they do not notice when they are much louder or softer.

When you realize what is going on, you can do something about the situation. When you notice a big difference in volume, close the gap by adjusting your own volume to match the other person's. When you have enough mutual trust, you can turn to other things and let the volume take care of itself.

Pitch. Some people sing bass, others sing soprano. Speaking voices also range from low to high. Matching pitches is one way to connect with other people. If you can sing with a musical instrument, you know how to do it. You hear a note from the piano, then sing that note. You can talk the same way. Listen for another person's tone and start talking on the same pitch.

Kevin Barber's secretary told him he sounded like a different person each time he spoke on the telephone. Kevin had practiced matching pitches. He would start talking on the same note the other person had finished on. The practice soon became a habit, and Kevin had many telephone voices.

The telephone presents a unique situation. You can use only your sense of hearing to receive messages and your ability to make sounds to send messages. Despite the AT&T song, you cannot literally "reach out and touch someone" long distance. The telephone's popularity, however, testifies to its effectiveness as a communication medium. You can build mutual trust by telephone with any of the methods which involve hearing:

- Speak their language.
- Listen to them.
- Match any of these signs:
  Voice expressions
  Breathing
  Pet words and phrases.
- Join their team.

Posture

Matching posture, or any of the other signs, is like a game of Follow the Leader. You start out following someone else and, if all goes well, you reach a point where it is hard to tell the leader from the follower. It should go well if you are subtle and natural in your following. Avoid exaggeration or anything else that might attract attention. People tend to get angry when they think they are being mocked.

Movements

People move all sorts of things from foot to forehead. One person can usually match what another can move. Watch people talking, walking or eating together. Notice how often their movements seem to be synchronized.

You can match movements by walking in step, blinking when others blink or tapping your toe when they tap their toes. Or you can do something else at the same time they move, such as tapping your finger when they tap their toes, rubbing your arm when they rub their noses or nodding when they breathe.

Breathing

A person may not talk. She may sit in a position you would not dare match. She may not even move. But everybody breathes. When you match breathing, you can be subtle and increase the trust level at the same time.

Some people's breathing is easier to follow than others'. Some do not seem to breathe at all, and some wear bulky clothing. You will usually see breathing patterns, but sometimes you can hear them. Remember, breathing can show up anywhere between collar bones and hip bones, so if you stare at a person's chest, you might miss his breathing. Be patient; some people do'nt seem to breathe very often or very deeply. The more you practice, the keener your eye becomes. Watch for shoulders rising and falling. Keep your ears open, and listen for the way a person pauses for breath while talking.

Pet Words and Phrases

Suppose a person says things like "that's an *excellent* idea," "I had an *excellent* lunch," and "he has an *excellent* memory." When you present an idea for that person's approval, do you describe it as (A) swell, (B) nice, (C) *excellent*, or (D) fantastic?

People show and tell you their pet words and phrases. By choosing words that people use frequently and emphasize with their voices and bodies, you are saying, "I heard what you said." This gives them a feeling that you understand them and that they understand you. After all, you speak the same language.

You can choose from millions of words in many languages, so why not pick the ones your listeners know and understand? Notice people's pet words, and use them.

Get on Their Side

Think about the terms, "face-to-face" and "side-by-side." Did you ever hear of a side-by-side confrontation? Side-by-side is a position of friendship or alliance. Chapter 7 spoke of getting on "their" side in a figurative sense. And good way to build trust is to literally stand or sit beside people. When you have the chance, sit beside them rather than on the "opposite" side.

The figurative approach works, too. The idea of having a common TARGET, especially when it's *their* TARGET, certainly builds trust. Letting other people know you are on their side and working to get what they want may build all the trust and comfort you need.

Mutual Trust Review

Here are some techniques you can use to build mutual trust. One list is for in-person conversations and the other is for use on the telephone.

In Person

- Speak their language.
- Listen to them.
- Match
    Voice expressions.
    Posture.
    Movements.
    Breathing.
    Pet words and phrases.
- Get on their side.

Telephone

- Speak their language.
- Listen to them.
- Match
    Voice expressions.
    Breathing.
    Pet words and phrases.
- Get on their side.

Remember: (1) Unless you trust others to do what you want them to in a situation, these techniques will do no good. (2) If you have mutual trust, you do not need the techniques. (3) If you do not have mutual trust, make it your top priority.

> He did not mean to show it, I am sure,
> but it was so strongly in his mind
> that it peeped out at every action.
> *Sherlock Holmes*

> He read the thought upon my features, and
> his smile had a tinge of bitterness.
> *Dr. Watson*

12

USE YOUR CLUES

Just before Christmas in 1986 the world's imagination was captured by the flight of Dick Rutan and Jeana Yeager in *Voyager*. This was the first time anyone had flown an airplane around the world nonstop without refueling.

Rutan and Yeager knew they had reached their TARGET when they heard and felt the engine shut off at Edwards Air Force Base. They saw a signal from a man outside the plane to shut off the engine. They knew Edwards Air Force Base when they saw it, because they had landed there many times. They found Edwards Air Force Base by following radio signals and other navigation aids. They knew they were ready to take off by the way the plane responded to test flights. They knew... But that's enough of that. Throughout the planning, development, and flight of *Voyager* the people involved had specific things to look, listen, and feel for which told them they were ON TARGET.

The first key clue came in 1981 when Dick's brother, Burt Rutan, suggested they build and airplane and fly around the world on one load of fuel. Dick had heard Burt say similar things before, "and a lot of them were joking... He would always wear a little smile, the corners of his mouth just turned up a bit. But this time I looked at his face, and the corners of his mouth were completely level. I looked into his eyes, and I could see he was dead-nuts serious."

For *Voyager* to become a real TARGET, Dick Rutan knew his brother must be in a serious mood, not joking.

USE YOUR CLUES

He compared Burt's face as he saw it with a picture in his mind of his brother joking. When he saw they didn't match, Dick was ready to go ahead with the project.

Dick Rutan knew exactly where to look: first the corners of his brother's mouth, then his eyes. Of all the possible clues, he checked two—the only ones he needed. Long ago he had eliminated the others as irrelevant.

When you are able to identify and recognize key clues like that, you can

- Steer toward your TARGET more accurately.
- Detect another person's shifting moods and attitudes toward your TARGET almost instantly, so you can respond quickly and appropriately.
- Notice when someone agrees to what you want, so you can act on it now and avoid missing out.

When driving to an airport, I look for the signs which guide me to the airport. "Airport Ahead" tells me I'm on the right road going in the right direction, so I continue. At "Airport Next Exit" I turn at the next exit. At "Airport Parking" I park. The signs tell me how I'm doing and what turns I need to take.

A few times I drove to an airport, did not see the sign I wanted, and went on through and out the other side. Usually two or three times around the circuit were enough to find my TARGET sign. Nobody ran out and hung up the sign after my second trip through. The sign was there all the time. I just didn't see it.

A large part of getting the results you want is

- Knowing the the signals you need to stay ON TARGET.
- Noticing the signals you get.
- Recognizing the signals you need when you get them.

By the time you get to this point in the process, you have reference clues in mind. You know what your TARGET looks, sounds, and feels like, the signals from other people which indicate you are getting warmer or cooler, and the ones which let you know you have hit that TARGET.

You can use your clues by noticing the signals you get from others, comparing them with ones you have stored for reference, and adjusting the messages you send accordingly.

Chapter 13 takes up the subject of what to do if you get signals indicating you are cool or cold. Chapter 14 goes into what to do when you get hot.

But first *you must* notice *the signals you get, and you must* recognize *the ones you need*. If you wanted to sell a house, you would probably realize it was sold when you transferred the deed and deposited the check. Those are definite signals, but they are not the first ones available. The words, "We'll take it," are also strong signals, but they also come late in the game. Before you hear them, you, or your agent, will see and hear many other signals. Will you notice them?

During World War II an Army draftee picked up every piece of paper he saw, looked at it, said, "That's not it," and threw it down. The company commander called the soldier into his office. While the commander explained that this behavior had to stop, the soldier picked up every paper on the captain's desk, looked at it, said, "That's not it," and threw it down. The captain sent the soldier to the psychiatrist, who gave the soldier a thorough psychological examination. During the examination, the soldier picked up every paper in the office, looked at it, said, "That's not it," and threw it down. After the examination, the psychiatrist said, "I'm not sure what your problem is, but it makes you unfit for military service. We'll have to discharge you." He filled out a discharge form and handed it to the draftee, who looked at it, said, "That's it!" and walked out.

Use Clues Review

Use the clues you get from others to guide you to your TARGET by
- Knowing which signals will lead you to your TG.
- Noticing the signals you get and using them to steer by.
- Recognizing the signals you need when you get them.

> It may be necessary to go south
> for a while in order to
> journey north.
> *Edward de Bono*
>
> "Doc, it hurts when I do this."
> "Then don't do that!"
> *Old Joke*

13

LOOSEN UP—TAKE ANOTHER APPROACH

A man called a locksmith and said he locked his keys in his car. The locksmith said he'd be there in about an hour. The man said, "Could you hurry. It looks like rain, and the top is down."

Most people in that situation could figure out some way to get those keys. But that story is just an exaggeration of a common condition. Few of us would lock the keys in a convertible, but how many get trapped into thinking we have only one choice of action in certain situations? As Bruce Lee put it,

> Because one does not want to be disturbed, to be made uncertain, he establishes a pattern of conduct, of thought, a pattern of relationships to man. He then becomes a slave to the pattern and takes the pattern to be the real thing.

Perhaps we can take an intelligent approach. Lee went on to say,

> Intelligence is sometimes defined as the capacity of the individual to adjust himself successfully to his environment—or to adjust the environment to his needs.

To put it simply:

If At First You Don't Succeed, Do Something Else.

Thomas Edison wanted to make an electric light bulb. To do that he needed a glowing filament. After testing a thousand materials, Edison had not found one which glowed. Someone asked if he was discouraged, and Edison replied that he was

closer to the solution than he had ever been, because he knew a thousand things that didn't work.

If Edison had stuck with the first material he tried, we would be watching television by the light of kerosene lamps today. But Edison was a bright man, and he did something else — more than a thousand times — until he got the electric light bulb he wanted.

According to Stafford Beer, "What matters in communication is what you end up with, not what you said or did." To end up with the results you want, you need to send messages most likely get those results. You can have good intentions, you can have great style, you can have flawless logic, but they don't matter unless you get the results.

You are most likely to hit your TARGET when you

- Know your TARGET (Chapter 6, Chapter 8).
- Aim for a mutually-beneficial outcome (Chapter 7).
- Have resourceful attitudes (Chapter 10).
- Have mutual trust (Chapter 11).
- Utilize feedback (Chapter 12).
- Avoid traps (Chapter 9, Chapter 18).
- Make it easy for others to understand and respond.

Ashby's Law says that the one with more choices of action in a situation controls that situation. Take Bugs Bunny for example. Though many creatures, human and otherwise, have used all sorts of tricks, traps, and tools attempting to kill, capture or cook this cartoon hero, the resourceful rodent outwitted them all.

There is no way we can cover everything you might do in every situation — or in any one situation. What we can do is consider a few general approaches you might not ordinarily think of.

What is the Situation?

There are many ways to get to Manhattan, but you can't choose the most effective way until you know where you are now. You can take the ferry from Staten Island, but not from The Bronx. You can take a train from Queens, but not from Marakesh or Madrid.

If you aren't getting results you want, run through this check list.

- Do you have a clear TARGET in mind?
- Are you dealing with the right person?

- Are you in a resourceful attitude?
- Is the other person in a resourceful attitude?
- Do you have mutual trust?
- Are you proposing something which is in that person's best interest?
- Are you sure you are interpreting the signals accurately? Could you be ON TARGET without realizing it?

When you have covered all those and still get signals that you are cool or cold, you can conclude that what you're doing is not working. That does not mean it will never work, but with that person under those conditions, it is not working. Then it is time to do something else.

What else should you do? That depends on the situation—what your TARGET is, who else is involved, and how you are relating to them. You can move the TARGET, adjust your aim, or adjust the way you send your message, whichever is appropriate.

When you do something else it either works or it doesn't. When it works you have what you wanted, and you can go on from there. If it doesn't work, you do something else again. As long as you have choices, you have a chance to succeed.

Following are some choices which can get you back ON TARGET.

HANDLING OBJECTIONS

You can expect that people will occasionally object to something you propose. Some people are afraid an objection signals the end of their chances. Others welcome objections as signs of interest and ways of asking for reasons to accept the proposal. Whether you want to propose marriage, negotiate a merger, or vacation in Hawaii, an objection can be a green light or a road block, depending on the way you handle it.

Some people turn objections into road blocks by ignoring them, arguing about them, or giving up. Here are some suggestions for turning those road blocks into green lights.

- First, Acknowledge the Objection.
- Use *and* instead of *but*.
- Use other words. Approach from another angle.
- Use surprise.
- Tell appropriate jokes or stories.

First, Acknowledge the Objection

People raise objections when they have legitimate concerns about things which could affect them. When those concerns are ignored, they stay where they are, blocking the road. If you change the subject, argue, or continue as if nothing happened, that person stays focused on that objection, and communication is stalled.

When you *let that person know you heard and understood the objection*, the process can move forward. The basic message to convey is this: "I understand that you are concerned about this, and I want to resolve it to your satisfaction." This defuses possible hostilities, maintains team spirit, and frees the other person to move on toward a mutually satisfactory conclusion.

Your exact words, gestures or expressions will depend on the person, the situation, the objection, and your own personality. Here are some examples.

"That's a good question."
"I'm glad you brought that up."
"I can understand your concern about that."
"In your position I would probably feel the same way."

You can also repeat the objection as a question, ask the other person to repeat it, or say something like, "If I understand correctly, you don't want the French fries that come with the meal. Is that right?"

Let the person know you know, then deal with the objection in a way that seems appropriate.

Nip It In The *but*

One thing to avoid in that situation is the three-letter word *but*. Many people do a fine job of acknowledging the objection, then promptly throw away their gains. It's like hitting a home run and being called out for passing the runner ahead of you. How many times have you heard something like this?

"That's a good question, but our statistics show..."
"I understand how you could be concerned about that,
    but our management believes..."
"Yes, they do require 220 volts, but our engineers..."

What has happened? The team spirit, the flow of communication, the ease of interaction has been nipped in the *but.* Often that word has the effect of cancelling what went before it.

"You're a nice guy, *but* here's your ring back."
"Your work has been fine, *but* we're letting you go."
"Yes, I see your point, *but* you don't know the facts."
"Yes, that's probably true, *but* not in this business."

The form "Yes, but..." is generally taken to mean, "You're right. No, you're wrong." Listen to some of the network TV news people interviewing public figures. After the public figure makes a statement, the interviewer often starts with, "*But...*" and sounds as if he's calling the person a liar.

But what can you say to maintain good relations when you do not agree with what the other person said? You can acknowledge the objection as a serious concern, and you can indicate that there may be other ways of considering the matter. You can do this by replacing the conjunction *but* with another three-letter word, *and*.

"Yes, I can see how you would be concerned about that, *and* our experience has been..."
"Yes, it does sound complicated, *and* those who use it say..."
"That's a good question, *and* our engineers feel..."

Notice what happens when other people say "Yes, *but...*" Then notice the difference when you say, "Yes, *and...*"

In Other Words

The words *but* and *and* can make a big difference in the effect of your message. The other words you use can also affect it. Based on our experiences, we all have individual meanings for words, and we have evaluated many words as good, bad, pleasant, unpleasant, great or awful. When we hear one of those words, we respond to that evaluation.

It is possible, then, to have a perfectly acceptable idea and to present it in words which draw an unfavorable reaction—or to present it in a way others don't understand. When this happens, we have another opportunity to do something else. In other words, we can put the idea into other words which might be more acceptable.

Some words work better with any one person than others do. If you notice your words aren't working, use some other words.

The idea of eating fish eggs, raw fish, or snails does not appeal to many Americans, but some of them have paid well to eat caviar, sushi, and escargot. On the other hand, one creative couple cut calories from their meals by substituting one word. Instead of asking for butter or margarine, they say, "Would you please pass the fat?"

Surprise

When we deal with people we have known a long time, we tend to get into routines as if we were following a script. Things follow a predictable pattern. If you don't like the results a pattern produces, break up the routine. You can lead the communication to another outcome by interrupting a pattern. That outcome may be more desirable than the routine one; it won't be the same.

When Michael Gardner found out he could interrupt the almost ritualistic patterns police officers find themselves in, he got more useful results.

The people police officers run into in domestic quarrels, robberies, and traffic violations, are likely to have negative, even belligerent reactions. When a police officer responds in a like manner, the pattern can quickly lead to violence.

Michael Gardner did something to prevent violence by interrupting this pattern before it got dangerous. Sometimes he and his partner would show up at the scene of a domestic quarrel with their caps down over their ears and their jackets buttoned wrong. Or in the midst of a quarrel, one of them would change the channel on the television set or sniff and say, "Do you smell gas?"

By doing the unexpected, Mike and his partner took people's attention from their own problems. How could they concentrate on a quarrel when these cops were doing such uncoplike things? How can a person respond when he tells a cop, "I can whip your butt!" and the cop replies, "I'll bet you can, but I sure don't want to find out"? He has to take time out to rethink the situation. This scene is not going according to the script.

Mike's wife, Debbie Gardner, conducts self-defense workshops, and she recommends doing the unexpected, to interrupt the usual pattern. When you do something you are not expected to do, others find it difficult to respond the way they expected to.

That reminds me

Jokes interrupt patterns. The setup gets the listeners going in one direction, then the punch line snaps them back in an unexpected direction. In appropriate circumstances jokes can serve several purposes at once. They can interrupt patterns and send the communication in another direction. They can increase the trust and comfort level of a conversation. They can shift people's attitudes and increase their breathing (when they laugh). Jokes, stories and analogies can often get a point across faster and easier than detailed explanations.

A story will do the job if the listeners can understand the connection between the story and the point you want to make. Some fine salespeople, teachers and psychotherapists seem to spend all their time telling stories, but their customers, students and clients get the message.

The Perfect Story

At a workshop in San Francisco in 1984 I was explaining the advantages of telling stories to get a point across. I seemed to be doing fairly well until Jim, a young business man, said he could not behave that way. He believed in plain, straightforward talk that came right to the point. He considered the more indirect approach of stories, jokes and metaphors to be unfair.

What I was doing didn't work with Jim, so I did several other things, which also made no impression. Others took up the cause and had the same effect.

As I wondered what would get Jim to realize the value of telling stories to promote understanding, the room was silent.

Then a rich baritone voice said, "Who is my neighbor? A man went down from Jerusalem to Jericho and fell among thieves."

That's all he said, but in a moment Jim understood what we had been trying to explain for fifteen minutes.

Ray Waetjen, a chaplain at the University of Oregon, had talked with Jim several times and knew enough about him to use the words he did. Ray concluded that those two sentences would remind Jim of the story of The *Good Samaritan,* remind him the story came from a source he respected, and remind him that the story is one of the parables which have been used for two thousand years to explain unfamiliar ideas.

Now I had the perfect story to demonstrate how useful and effective telling stories can be—I thought. But I missed a critical point which, naturally, came up when I told that story at the next workshop. As I finished, a woman said, "I don't understand. What does that mean?"

Stories can be extremely effective, *but only when they fit into the listener's frame of reference.*

Kenneth Bailey compares the parables with a political cartoon, which uses symbols the majority of its readers will interpret correctly. "The storyteller, in the telling of the parable, skillfully uses these symbols to press the original listener to make a single decision/response."

By describing one thing in terms of another, we can teach or explain unfamiliar ideas by associating them with familiar ones.

"There's More Than One Way..."

In 1948 Harrison Dillard was the best high hurdler in the world, and his TARGET was an Olympic gold medal. Unfortunately, he did not qualify for the Olympic team as a hurdler. But Harrison Dillard had two other angles. He qualified and won the gold medal in the 100-meter dash in 1948, and he won the gold medal in the hurdles in 1952.

Another Approach Review

The message of this chapter is simple. **If at first you don't succeed, do something else.** As long as you have choices, you are still in the game. And with realistic TARGETS, you usually have choices as long as your imagination and your patience hold out.

What else specifically? That depends on the situation, and here are a few suggestions.
- Acknowledge all objections.
- Use *and*, not *but*.
- If your message doesn't get across, use other words.
- Use surprise to interrupt patterns and get other results.
- Make your points with jokes or stories.

TAKE YES

FOR AN ANSWER

> Don't whip your horse after
> he's passed the finish line.
> *Fibber McGee*
>
> When the iron is hot, strike.
> *John Heywood*

14

TAKE YES FOR AN ANSWER

Madge Hart, will not take yes for an answer. Every evening she asks her husband Dan what he wants for dinner, and Dan replies, "I don't care. It's all good." Then Madge recites a menu. "Spaghetti?" Dan says, "That sounds good. Let's have spaghetti." But Madge says, "We could have tacos." Dan says, "Good. Let's have tacos." But Madge goes on to list four other possibilities, and Dan agrees to three of them.

That sort of thing seldom happens in restaurants. As soon as a customer makes a selection, the waiter takes the menu away and starts the next step — getting the food prepared.

What has Madge accomplished? She reached her TARGET with one question, then passed by it with five more. She threw her "bird in hand" back into the bush.

We hear of people who won't take no for an answer, but we don't hear much about those who won't take *yes* for an answer.

Everything in the book to this point has been to prepare you for hitting a specific TARGET. Yet many people do not know what to do when they succeed. An amazing number will not take yes for an answer. Maybe they are not used to succeeding and find themselves in unfamiliar territory. Perhaps they don't expect to succeed or they don't plan that far ahead. Some have a long list of reasons, evidence and persuasive material, and they don't want to quit until they have used them all.

Perhaps the main reason so many people miss out on TARGETS they have hit is that they are not paying attention to signals and don't realize they have the result they want. Getting there may be half the fun, but you can go too far. And if you go too far, getting there may be all the fun you have.

there may be half the fun, but you can go too far. And if you go too far, getting there may be all the fun you have.

Jim Treat sold radio advertising for several years, and he knew how to recognize signals which told him the time was ripe to close a sale. He also realized that receptive condition only lasts a short time. No matter how much presentation Jim might have prepared, he knew that if he kept "selling," he could kill the sale. He had to shift to another gear, get the contracts signed and get information for the commercial messages.

When the iron in a blacksmith's forge is hot enough, it is malleable and he can put that iron on an anvil and hammer it into any shape he wants. When it cools he can no longer do that, so he must strike while the iron is hot.

The Last Place We Look

Why do we find things in the last place we look?

When I lose my car keys, I retrace my steps from the last time I drove. I shake clothing I wore and listen for keys jingling. At some point I find those keys and it turns out to be the last place I look, because then I quit looking for keys and go out to drive the car.

I know I found the keys because when I saw, heard or felt them, I *recognized* them. Blacksmiths recognize the red color of hot iron. By now you know what your TARGET will look and sound like. When you see or hear it, *recognize it!* Utilize your feedback to find out when you're hot.

When you are hot, quit doing what you were doing and do something else. Take the next logical step toward what you really want. Sign the contracts, buy the marriage license, deposit the check, or serve the food.

Be Prepared for a Bonus

Sometimes reality exceeds our imagination. When that happens, most people accept it and enjoy it. But some are so tightly focused on what they are expecting that they will actually turn down a better deal.

Paul Price wants to fly from Atlanta to Phoenix. He bought a Super-Super-Saver ticket well in advance, and now he is at the Atlanta airport. He discovers his flight has been over-booked, and even though he had a seat reserved, someone else is sitting in it. The airline representative offers to seat him in the first class section at no extra charge, but Paul insists on sitting in the crowded coach seat he paid for.

Can you imagine someone actually doing that? I know people who have taken the first class seat with no fuss, but I have not heard of anyone who turned down a deal like that. However, I would not be surprised if someone did. Some people get so focused on one thing that they won't accept something even better.

To avoid missing out on the extras that life offers from time to time, you must be able to recognize a better deal for what it is, and you must realize unexpected bonuses can turn up.

The airplane deal is easy. Almost anybody will realize the TARGET is to get to the destination, and a first class seat at the same price will serve that purpose is just as well as the Super-Super-Saver coach seat. Some choices are less obvious, however. You might be aiming for a promotion to assistant manager, but the company offers to promote you to manager—of the Wichita branch. Is this a better deal? Only you can decide that. It depends on your circumstances—the salary, your personal situation, whether you are in Salina or San Francisco, and other factors you must consider.

When you're offered a better deal than you expected, take it.

Connie Cook asked her husband, Claude, "Would you like spaghetti for dinner?"
Claude said, "Yes. That sounds good."
And Connie said, "OK. We'll have spaghetti."
So she fixed spaghetti, and they lived happily all evening.

Take Yes Review

Recognize your TARGETS when you reach them.

When you recognize the signs you're looking and listening for, take yes for an answer. Quit "persuading" and get on with the next step.

Be prepared for unexpected bonuses.

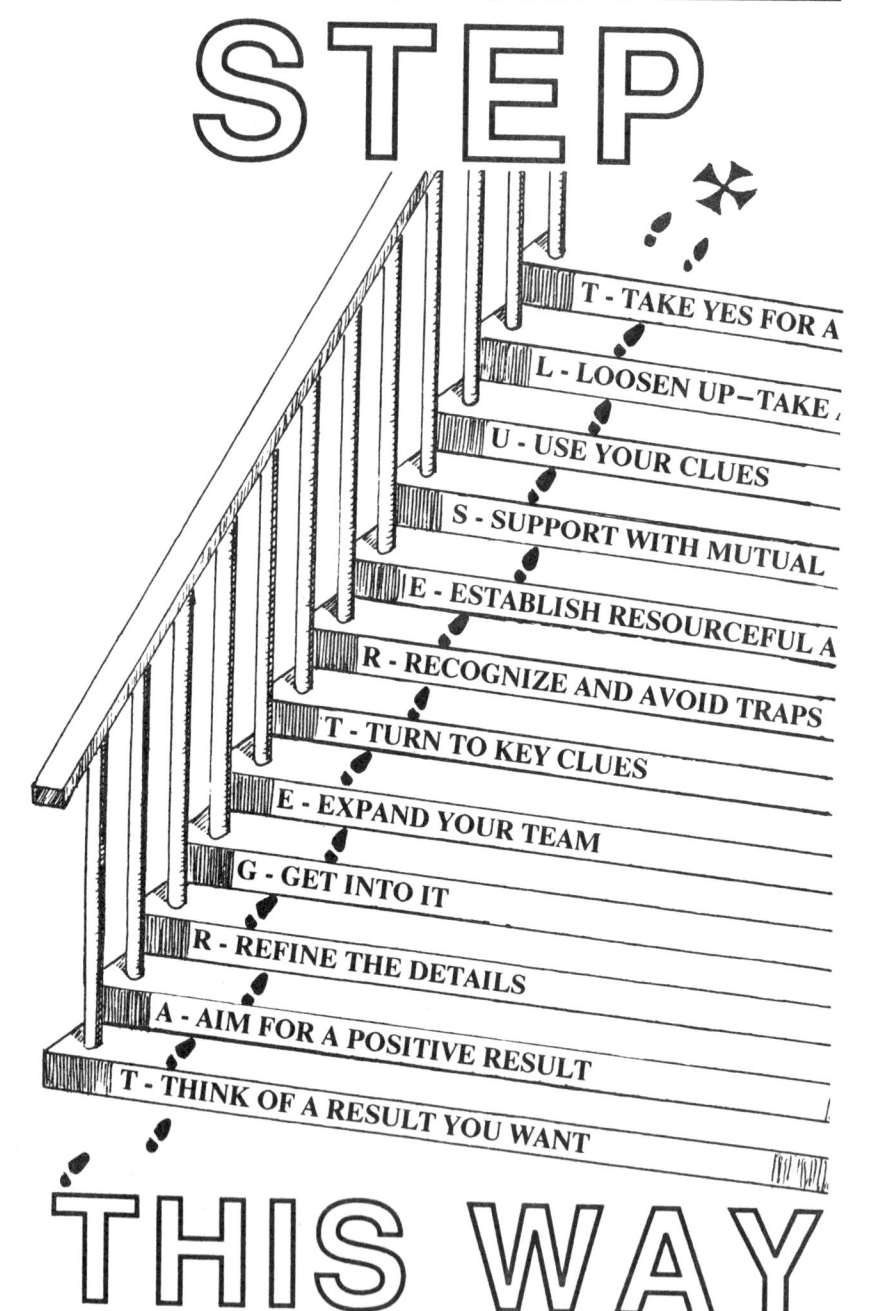

> Take what is useful and
> develop from there.
> *Bruce Lee*

15

STEP THIS WAY

It turns out that Bert Baron from Chapter 5 really did want a new office building, and he had a pretty good idea what he wanted. He remembered things he liked about various buildings he had visited, and he put them together in a mental model, which he tested and liked. Then, after making sure they were both in resourceful attitudes and had enough mutual trust, Bert described the building to Lisa Alexander, the architect.

Lisa drew plans and sketches, and she told Bert what would work and what wouldn't. When all the wrinkles were ironed out, Bert took the plans to Mark Mason, the contractor. Once again Bert made sure they were in resourceful and trusting attitudes. They quickly negotiated a contract at a price they both considered fair. They knew what the finished building looked like, and when it looked like that, Mason construction quit building. Bert settled his account and moved into the building.

This story isn't particularly dramatic or amusing. I didn't intend for it to be. Dramas, and comedies, need some kind of conflict to provide tension, suspense, and adversity to overcome. But we're here to simplify matters and to avoid conflicts and unnecessary complications.

A journey of a thousand miles ends with a single step. And so does any other journey. Our journey toward your TARGETS ends with this step, which is a summary of the previous twelve.

The steps are listed on the previous page, and following is a check list. As you set up TARGETS and go for results you want, you can clarify your thinking by asking yourself the questions on the following page.

TARGET AND RESULTS CHECK LIST

1. What do you want?
2. Is it something under your control?
3. Is it a positive accomplishment, something you want to have, do or be?
4. What will you see, hear and feel when you have the result you want?
5. How does it feel when you mentally test it?
6. Do you really want it?
7. Who else is involved?
8. What do they want?
9. How can you overlap your TARGET with theirs?
0. Is it worth the time and effort you must invest?
11. What signs from them will let you know you are warm, cool, hot or cold?
12. Will what you are going to do lead you into a trap?
13. Do you expect people to think or behave like you or someone else?
14. What attitude would be most effective for this situation?
15. Are you in that attitude now?
16. Are you breathing?
17. Are the other people attentive and responsive?
18. Do you have mutual trust?
19. What responses are you getting?
20. How do they compare with the responses you want?
21. Are you getting warmer or cooler?
22. If you are getting cooler, are you doing something else?
23. Are you acknowledging objections?
24. Are you saying *and* or *but*?
25. Are you taking yes for an answer?

PART 4

PARTING SHOTS

In Chapter 9 I mentioned riding a horse who would leave the other horses in the corral only by walking backward. I had no trouble getting her to return to the corral. As a matter of fact, she covered the ground rather quickly.

After an expedition through TARGETS and RESULTS, we are within sight of the corral, but we have a little more ground to cover before we get there. Much of the material in this section is in answer to requests for ways to develop techniques useful in carrying out some of the steps in Part 2 and Part 3, and for ways to use those steps for self-defense.

TARGET PRACTICE

Some of the techniques, such as noticing nonverbal signals and identifying key clues are easier and more useful when you have some experience with them. Chapter 16 gives you some games to play which can give you that kind of experience.

HANDLING MANIPULATION

Some people want to protect themselves from manipulation. Others are concerned that some of the techniques could be manipulative. Chapter 17 discusses several aspects of manipulation, self-defense, and ethics.

IN CONCLUSION

This chapter winds up our expedition and takes us back to the corral where you will be free to browse through the Sources and the Index—if you like to do that kind of thing.

TARGET

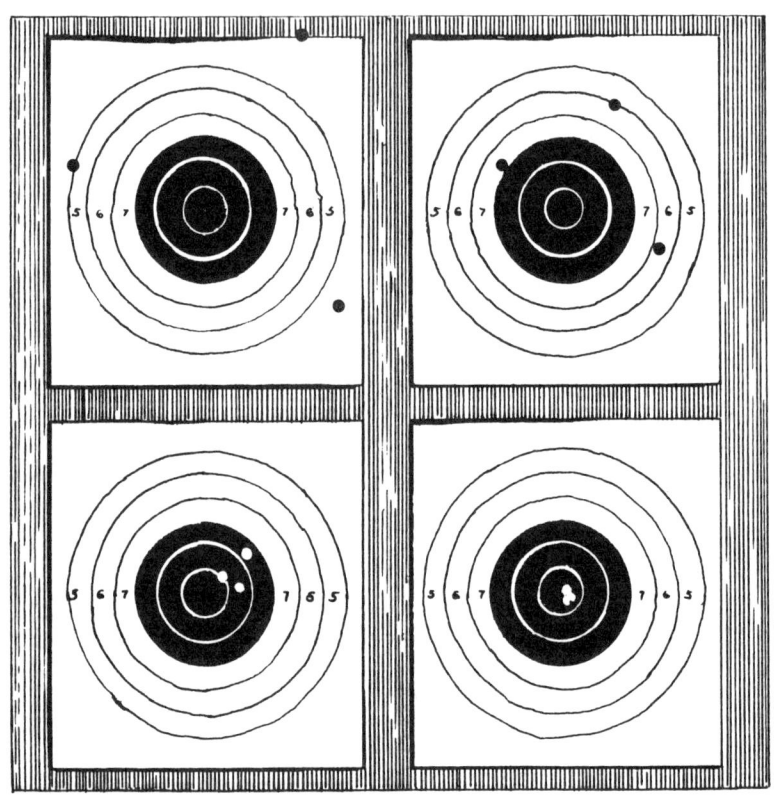

PRACTICE

> The battle of Waterloo was won
> on the playing fields of Eton.
> *The Duke of Wellington*

16

TARGET PRACTICE

The Expert badge I earned on the rifle range at Ft. Riley, Kansas, was a result of knowing what to do, knowing how to do it, and a lot of practice. I had prepared for that moment by practicing, off and on, for fifteen years.

You have been preparing to get results your whole life, although your practicing may not have been so clear-cut. You may not have realized that playing games builds confidence you can use in giving reports, or vice versa.

The things we do best are things we do automatically. In the motion picture, *The Karate Kid*, an old Okinawan man agreed to teach an American kid karate. But first he had the kid wash and wax four automobiles with specific circular motions. Then he had the kid sand a huge deck with circular motions. After that the kid painted an even larger fence with up-and-down motions.

While he was doing all that, the kid wondered when he would start learning karate. When he finished those chores, he discovered he was doing basic karate movements automatically. It was no accident that they were the same movements he had used to wash, wax, polish, sand, and paint.

You can develop skills in many ways. The important thing is that what you do must produce the results you want. If we can get those results by playing games, let's play games.

Some points in this book stand by themselves. Once you know them, you can use them. You can think of what you want, make it positive, etc. You can also improve your abilities in certain areas with directed activity. Some steps—such as noticing nonverbal signals—can definitely benefit from practical experience. You can develop these skills in several ways. One of the best ways is to attend a workshop or training program run by competent people. Until you get to that point, you can get some useful experience by playing the games in this chapter.

You can play these games with friends and relatives. Some you can do solo. Some you can play in 'real life' situations.

Game 1: What's the Difference?

A. Ask someone about a situation which will probably bring a shift of mood or attitude. For example, if the subject has been serious, ask about something lighter; if she has been talking about family, ask about work, hobby, or current events.
B. Each time you do this, focus on one source of visual information or tune in to a voice quality (Chapter 8).
C. Notice what happens as the mood shifts. Does what you are focused on shift? If so, how? Can you recognize it again?
D. You win this game when you can identify some reliable nonverbal indication of a particular attitude for that person.

Game 2: Drop the Dollar

With the experience of Game 1 under your belt, you're ready for a challenge. This one is impossible, a man on television said so. But I have done it, and you can, too.

A. You need another person and a piece of paper money. The other person holds one end of the bill between thumb and forefinger, and you hold your thumb and forefinger on either side of the other end of the bill, without touching it.
B. When he feels like it, the other person drops the bill.
C. You catch it between your thumb and forefinger before it passes through.
D. You win when you catch the bill five times in a row.
E. Then switch and let the other person catch it.

Game 3: Follow the Leader

As you play this game, notice what happens to you and to the people you follow.

A. Do B through F one at a time, then two at a time in various combinations. Then do three at a time.

B. While carrying on a conversation notice another person's breathing pattern. Breathe the same way that person breathes and at the same rate.
C. Notice the other person's posture. Match that posture. Do it naturally and don't attract attention.
D. Notice the other person's movements. Match those movements. Do it naturally and don't attract attention.
E. Notice the person's rate of speech. When you speak, speak at the same rate.
F. Notice the pitch of the person's voice. When you speak, speak in the same range of pitch.
G. Your objective is to do B through F comfortably and without being noticed.

Game 4: Lead the Leader

When you are comfortable with Game 3, add this wrinkle.

A. After you have been following a person's breathing, position, rate of speech, etc. for a few minutes, shift to another position, rate, etc.
B. Notice whether the other person follows you or not.
C. Your objective is to get the other person to follow your lead within 60 seconds.

Game 5: Twenty Questions Plus

A. Person A thinks of an object and tells whether it is animal, vegetable or mineral.
B. Person B asks questions which can be answered yes or no.
C. A answers the questions truthfully with either yes or no.
D. B listens to the answers and notices the nonverbal (Chapter 16) differences between the yes and no answers. B wins the round by guessing the object in twenty questions or less.
E. For the second round A thinks of another object and tells whether it is animal, mineral or vegetable.
F. B again asks yes-or-no questions.
G. A answers every question by saying "Blue."
H. B determines whether the answer is yes or no from the nonverbal clues.
I. In early rounds you may use the option of having A correct any inaccurate guesses.

Game 6: Radar

A. Choose a result you want, and determine what response you need from the other person to get that result. For example, an indication the person is pleased with a software program. This can be either a role-playing game or a real life situation.
B. Using methods from Chapter 8, or anything else you can think of, entice that person to demonstrate those responses.
C. Look and listen for shifts in nonverbal signals.
D. Your object is to identify at least one reliable signal for that response from that person.

Game 7: Hot or Cold

A. After you have successfully played Radar, start asking questions or giving information regarding the result you want.
B. Notice whether the responses you get are warm or cool.
C. When you get cool responses, adjust what you're doing.
D. Your object is to get the response you identified in Radar.

Game 8: Do It Again

A. If the response you got in Game 8 was not the one you wanted, say or do the same thing again.
B. Notice the response this time.
C. If you still don't get that response, do something else.
D. Your object is to adjust your messages until you get the response you want.

Game 9: Qualify

A. Select a result you want.
B. Decide whose side you need to be on to get that result.
C. Approach and qualify (Chapter 7) that person (either a role-player or a real person).
D. Your object is to qualify the person as quickly and smoothly as you can.

Game 10: Clear Signals

A. Select several moods or attitudes you would like to be able to clearly indicate nonverbally. For example, friendliness, understanding, good humor, seriousness, and confidence.
B. Ask another person to identify your moods from their nonverbal qualities.

C. Your object is for five people in a row to identify your moods.

Game 11: What Do They Want?

A: Find out what someone else (role-player or real) wants in relation to a TARGET you've selected. (See Chapter 7.)
B. Once you find out what that person wants, find out if that is what she *really* wants. (Chapter 6, Chapter 7)
C. Your object is to discover what the person really wants while maintaining a harmonious relationship. When you get good at this game, you should charge for the service, because most people are not aware of what they really want. They get hung up on intermediate goals like money, power and possessions.

Game 12: Draw a Face

Artists say you must see in order to draw. Like many other things, this works both ways. You can also draw in order to see.

A. Find someone who will sit still a while, Or look in a mirror.
B. Draw the face you see in as much detail as you can.
C. You don't necessarily need to draw a masterpiece. Your object is to focus on the details of the face until you can draw a reasonable likeness.

Game 13: I'm Number One

A. Select one aspect of your life, and analyze it. If you were the Number One person in that field, what would you be like? What do top people do? What would you do differently?
B. Make a complete list of the Number One behaviors.
C. Begin to behave that way.
D. Your object is to notice what happens when you act as if you are Number One.

Game 14: Objection

A. Propose some course of action to someone else (a role player or a real life person).
B. When that person objects, acknowledge the objection (Chapter 13).
C. Your object is to automatically recognize and acknowledge objections.

Game 15: and

A. Eliminate the word *but* from your vocabulary for three weeks. Whenever that word is about to come out, say "and" instead.
B. Notice the effect it has on you and on people you talk with.
C. Your object is to develop an alternative response to objections (Chapter 13).

Game 16: In Other Words

You can play this game by yourself or with others.

A. One person says something.
B. Another person re-states or comments on what the first person said in a way that re-states the idea from another angle. (Chapter 13).
C. Continue re-stating until someone is stuck. That person then starts back at A.
D. Your object is to find as many angles and ways of saying something as possible.

Game 17: I See What You're Saying

A. For a period of five minutes use only see words (Chapter 17) in a conversation.
B. For five minutes use only hear words (Chapter 17).
C. For five minutes use only feel words (Chapter 17).
D. For five minutes use only neutral words (Chapter 17).
E. Your object is to be able to identify and use see, hear, feel, and neutral words. If you play this as a game with others, their object is to catch the speaker using words other than the ones specified.

Game 18: Advanced I See What You're Saying

A. Carry on a conversation with someone, in a game or a real-life situation.
B. Notice the see, hear or feel words the other person uses.
C. Use the same types of words when you speak.
D. Your object is to match that sensory language as long as that person uses it. If the person switches to another type, You follow. In a game situation, the leader or an observer is to detect the times you don't match the language being used.

> When information is in the hands
> of just a few, you're at their
> mercy. You play by their rules.
> *AT&T Commercial*
>
> Do unto others as you would
> have them do unto you.
> *Jesus*

17

HANDLING MANIPULATION
Self-Defense and Ethics

From the time their children begin to talk until they leave home, most American parents hear things like

"I want a new bicycle."
"Let me stay up just a little later."
"May I please have another cookie?"
"Can I use the car tonight?"

If the parents' first response happens to be "No," the kids usually persist, either with more of the same or with other methods. These can include crying, flattery, "everybody else is doing it," and just doing it anyway. Children can be quite resourceful at finding and exploiting parents' weak spots.

We frequently call a child who does this sort of thing a little manipulator. Some little manipulators carry their techniques with them into adult life. Others acquire other methods. As a result, we find many adults who can and do manipulate people.

Now manipulation, like beauty, is in the eye, and feelings, of the beholder. It is also a matter of degree.

Everything we do *affects* the people we come in contact with to some extent. Most of these affects are not even noticeable. Some can lead to beneficial results for all parties, and others can lead to benefits for some and regrets for others. When a person's behavior results in winners and losers, it often falls into an area known as *manipulating*.

Where is the line between affecting and manipulating? It's — Oh, no, you don't! You can't manipulate me into drawing a line when its location depends on the situation and who's involved.

Since manipulation is determined by the beholder, notice responses. When people discover they have been manipulated, they tend to feel used, betrayed, swindled, suckered, or otherwise victimized. As a consequence manipulation has developed an unfavorable reputation.

Some people manipulate consciously and deliberately, some do it through force of habit, and others would never think of doing such a thing. They do it without thinking. However they do it, manipulators usually come out ahead and manipulatees lose something—money, time, self-respect, faith in people, etc.

Manipulators are found in all walks of life. Most of us have known, or known of, politicians, advertisers, managers, employees, friends, relatives and others who do not play fair.

This is nothing new. For thousands of years religions have advocated treating people fairly with standards like the Golden Rule, "Do unto others as you would have them do unto you."

But not everyone acts according to those standards. You have probably heard, "Do unto others before they do unto you," or the other golden rule, "The one with the gold makes the rules." So how can you handle manipulation?

That, of course, depends on the result you want.

> Do you want to manipulate others?
> Do you want to prevent others from manipulating you?
> Do you want to avoid manipulating others?

MANIPULATING OTHERS

If your purpose were to take unfair advantage of others so that you win and they lose—a J. R. Ewing-type approach—I would feel obliged to point out some disadvantages you might find.

At the end of the 1979-1980 season of *Dallas*, J. R. Ewing got shot, and super-market tabloids speculated for months on who did it. J. R. had done so many underhanded things to so many people that *everybody* in the cast was a likely suspect. Many who didn't shoot him tried other kinds of revenge.

Prisons are full of people who didn't think they would have to pay the consequences of an unfair, and illegal, advantage.

One disadvantage, then, is consequences—exposure to reprisal of some sort and spending otherwise needless time and money on means of protection.

Another disadvantage for many people is that they "can't fool all the people all the time." Repeat business, the life blood of most enterprises, is hard to come by when customers are dissatisfied. Not only do they refuse to come back, but they also tell others. This applies to buying and selling, of course, and it also applies to any other type of personal relationship. Some victims may take longer to catch on than others, but when they do, the consequences can be severe.

A Better Way

Chapter 7 pointed out what many people consider to be a better way to get results: find out what other people want and help them get it. This avoids the disadvantages mentioned above, and it makes your job much easier.

Of course following that path takes you from the area we are calling manipulation and into the realm of mutual benefits. Healthy business, personal, and international relationships have always been mutually beneficial.

Dangerous Tools

Teaming up for mutually beneficial results is a highly-effective method of reaching TARGETS which involve other people. That step makes the whole process more effective and efficient.

However, some people have been concerned about other steps. They say things like matching nonverbal signals to build mutual trust are, or can be manipulative. Some have said knowledge like this should not be make available to the public.

I agree that some of these methods might be used to manipulate. They might be dangerous in unscrupulous hands. We can say the same thing about most tools, mass media, and sources of energy. A screwdriver is extremely handy for driving and removing screws, yet some people use screwdrivers as weapons. Television, electricity, automobiles, the list is endless. But remember, the tools themselves are neither useful nor destructive until some human agency puts them into operation.

When an electric power line is down, people who know about such things take steps to avoid coming in contact with the wire and with any conductors it may be touching. People who don't know about them can get electrocuted.

How can we protect ourselves from manipulation if we don't know about potential tools for manipulators? That's a rhetorical question. We can't. So let's talk self-defense.

SELF-DEFENSE

Most of the processes described in this book have been in operation for thousands of years, although they have not been identified, collected, and organized in this specific form. The study of verbal and nonverbal communicating has increased in the past few years. University professors and Ph.D. candidates have done a lot of this investigating, but so have people in advertising agencies, political consultants, and other potential manipulators. These people want to find the words and images which will persuade you to buy or vote the way they want. Wouldn't it be nice if you recognized those signals when you were exposed to them?

By knowing about the methods in this book—what they are, how they work, and how to recognize them—you can prevent others from using them to take advantage of you.

"How could you do that?" said the judge to the convicted confidence man, "Swindle people who trusted you?"

"Well, judge," said the con man, "It's almost impossible to swindle people who *don't* trust you."

If you feel yourself leaning, literally or figuratively, toward someone's proposal, mentally step back and ask yourself if this is something you *really* want (Chapter 6). If it is, fine.

If you *don't* want what that person offers, you can either do something about getting what you do want, or you can quit the game. You can depart in several ways. One is to mentally check out and go somewhere else until the person is through. Many of us use this one during commercials which don't appeal to us. Another way is to check out physically—say, "I don't want that," and leave. Or leave without saying anything. Many people who have been unmercifully manipulated for years by long distance finally caught on and hung up on the perpetrator. Manipulation is a game you don't have to play.

Once you realize what is going on, you can choose to disengage or to use some of these techniques to bring about a more desirable outcome. If you choose this route, make sure you

- Have a clear TARGET in mind (Part 2).
- Notice your posture, breathe, and establish a resourceful attitude (Chapter 10).
- Have mutual trust (Chapter 11).
- Avoid traps (Chapter 9).
- Notice the clues you get and use them to guide your actions (Chapter 12).
- Do something else, if you don't succeed (Chapter 13).

This last point may be a key to much manipulation, and for two different reasons. (1) A manipulator with more choices of behavior and can stay at least one step ahead, or (2) when neither party seems to have any other choices, they repeat the routines they have been going through, in some cases for years.

The element of surprise (Chapter 13) can be especially useful for re-routing old routines. As Mike Gardner found out, people just can't stay in their regular patterns when somebody else comes up with a new script.

Remember the idea from Chapter 7 that your objective in any situation is to help other people hit their TARGETS *only* when that will also hit your TARGET. A fair exchange is what you're after. And only you can decide if it's fair for you. A good feeling can be a fair exchange. A bad feeling usually isn't.

TO AVOID MANIPULATING OTHERS

You cannot avoid influencing other people's responses when you are around them. You can control the way you influence them—when you know what you are doing.

One man actually said, "I know I manipulate, but I don't want to know how I do it. Then I won't be responsible." This man, by the way, was a lawyer, and I wonder if he would have the same attitude toward the defendant if his client were the plaintiff in a negligence case.

You can avoid manipulating by making sure you are on their side to hit their TARGET (Chapter 7). This seems to be getting repetitious, but it still works. Only someone deep in the contrariness trap (Chapter 9) would complain about getting something he really wanted. In most cases the Crawford Consideration (Chapter 7) will take you a long way toward dealing fairly by assuring that what you do is in others' best interest. Another version of the Golden Rule is: Do unto others as *they* would have you do unto them.

Knowing the steps in this book—what they are, how they work, and how to use them can help you be more ethical than you might otherwise be. That knowledge lets you take steps to avoid manipulating and still improve your results.

PERSONAL VALUES

One idea behind this book is that knowing how humans communicate helps you improve your results. With this knowledge you can take the initiative. You get better results by getting on another person's side than by waiting for her to come to yours. You get mutual trust quicker by acting like someone else than by waiting for him to act like you.

These are practical matters, and sometimes practical matters conflict with personal values. How far should you go in joining someone else?

In Woody Allen's movie, *Zelig,* the title character was so insecure as a child that he developed a chameleon-like ability to look, sound and act like any other person. That may be going too far, because when he did that, there was very little of Zelig left, especially when he got into a Black jazz band.

Fortunately, you can communicate effectively and still keep your own identity. Remember, that identity has several facets and can adapt to a variety of situations. You can dress up or be casual when appropriate. You can speak formally or informally. You can match someone else's voice tone or posture without compromising your personal integrity. .

Remember, also, that this book deals with form and process, not content. You can choose to participate or not. You can acknowledge an objection without agreeing with it. You can understand how a person can think a certain way without thinking that way yourself.

Only you can decide where your limits are. Chapter 6 can help with that by letting you experience your TARGET and its down-the-line consequences. And Chapter 7 lets you find out what teaming up with someone else will cost, not only in time, effort or money, but also in psychic strain and self-esteem. With a clear TARGET (Part 2) and a resourceful attitude (Chapter 10) you can be fair to others and to yourself.

Manipulation Summary

It is in your best interest to avoid manipulation—either manipulating others or allowing them to manipulate you. You can prevent both by knowing how people affect each other and by noticing what goes on. The more you know about the ways we communicate, the more you can protect yourself from those who would take unfair advantage. The more you develop mutually-beneficial results, the more you realize this is an easier, safer, more effective way to get what you want and still be true to your own principles.

> Our remedies oft in ourselves do lie.
> Shakespeare

18

IN CONCLUSION

In India residents of the village of Nana had a TARGET: to be able to produce enough food to feed themselves. But this village had three big liabilities—it had too many people, its fields were full of rocks, and the land was dry as a bone, except for the annual monsoon floods. So, despite having a TARGET, the situation in Nana was hopeless.

Then Raja Ram Gupta, a wealthy industrialist, presented the people of Nana with a plan for reaching their TARGET by putting their assets to work. What assets? The people, the rocks, and the monsoon floods. The people carried the rocks out of the fields and build dams in dry river beds. When the rains came, the dams held water which the people used to irrigate the rock-free fields. Within a few years Nana had extra food to sell.

Personal traits, characteristics, abilities, and talents can be assets or liabilities, depending on our attitudes toward them and how we use them. Sometimes we need an outside point of view—someone who can tell us what our real assets are. Roger Ailes says you have everything you need to be an effective communicator. And communicating is the way to get results.

You've been communicating all your life. In this book I wanted to point out some assets you may not have been aware of and to suggest ways of utilizing them so you can give some direction to what you are already doing so you can get results on purpose rather than by accident. To do this, set up a clear TARGET, avoid shooting yourself in the foot, and treat the other people involved as individuals.

You can do it. The system works for almost any situation you will encounter—if you use it. My experience indicates that you will be more apt to follow these steps when you have a positive attitude. The answers we get depend on the questions we ask, and after noticing how well these steps work, I realized I was asking another question. I used to ask, "Will I do this." Now I *ask*, "*How* will I do it? and get more productive answers.

I wonder how you'll improve your results. That depends on what you want, of course, and that's where I came in. Before we part company, though, let's hit the main points one more time.

- Everything we do gets results.
- Everything we do sends messages.
- We get results by sending and receiving messages.
- The meaning of any message is the response it gets.
- To improve your results, improve your communicating.
- Know what you want—set up a TARGET.
  Think of a result you want.
  Aim for a positive result.
  Refine the details. What will you see, hear, and feel?
  Get into it. Find out if this is what you *really* want.
  Expand your team—hit *their* TARGET to also hits yours.
  Turn to key clues to keep you ON TARGET.
- Keep your TARGET in mind as you follow these steps:
  Recognize and Avoid traps.
  Establish resourceful Attitudes in yourself and others.
  Support the process with Mutual Trust.
  Use key clues—find out if you're off base or ON TARGET.
  Loosen up. If you don't succeed, do something else.
  Take *yes* for an answer.
- Knowing these steps and how they work can help protect yourself.
  Notice the processes others use.
  What's in it for you.
  If the exchange isn't fair, don't play.
  If it's fair you're better off helping others get what they want.
- You have all you need to improve your results.
- As a knowledgeable communicator you can do things to get results
- Attitude is everything. *How* will you reach your TARGET?

BEFORE (Random)

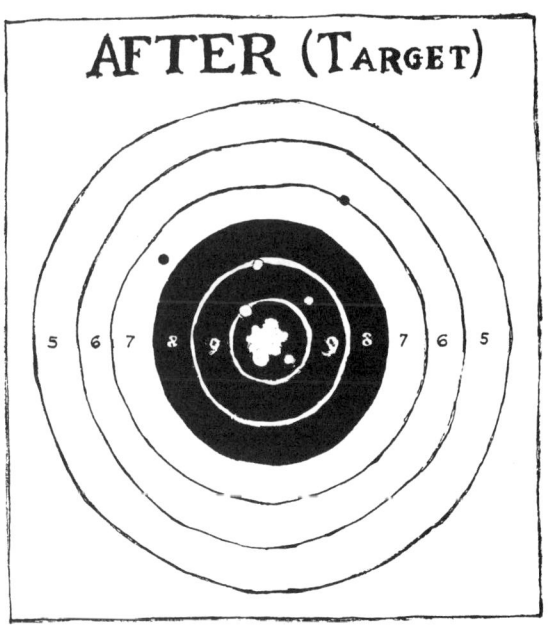

SOURCES

Adams, L. J. *Intermediate Algebra.* New York. Henry Holt, 1954.
Adams, Douglas. *So Long, And Thanks for All the Fish.* New York. Pocket Books, 1984.
Ailes, Roger. *You Are the Message: Secrets of the Master Communicators.* Homewood, Illinois. Dow-Jones Irwin, 1988.
Andreas, Connirae and Steve Andreas. *Change Your Mind—and Keep the Change.* Moab, Utah. Real People Press, 1987.
Ashby, W. Ross. *An Introduction to Cybernetics.* London. Methuen and Company, Ltd. 1979.
Associated Press. "Humor in uniform is working for clowning Cincinnati Cops." *Lincoln Journal-Star.* November 13, 1988.
Bailey, Kenneth E. *Poet and Peasant and Through Peasant Eyes.* Grand Rapids, Michigan. William B. Eerdmans Publishing Company, 1983.
Bailey, Rodger. *The Language and Behavior Profile Manual.* Dallas. BALI Screening Company, Inc., 1986.
Bandler, Richard and John Grinder. *The Structure of Magic.* Palo Alto, California. Science and Behavior Books, 1975.
Bandler, Richard and John Grinder. *Frogs into Princes.* Moab, Utah. Real People Press, 1979.
Bateson, Gregory. *Steps to an Ecology of Mind.* New York. Ballentine Books, 1972.
Beer, Stafford. *Brain of the Firm.* Chichester. John Wiley and Sons, 1981..
Beer, Stafford. *Heart of Enterprise.* Chichester. John Wiley and Sons, 1979.
Beer, Stafford. *Platform for Change.* Chichester. John Wiley and Sons, 1978.
Biggers, Earl Derr. *Charlie Chan Carries On.* New York. Grosset and Dunlap, 1930.
Brandreth, Gyles. *Your Vital Statistics.* Secaucas, New Jersey. Citadel Press, 1986.
Carnegie, Dale. *How to Win Friends and Influence People.* New York. Pocket Books, 1964.
Christie, Agatha. *The Mysterious Mr. Quin.* New York. Dell Publishing, 1969.
Coren, Stanley, Clare Porac, and Lawrence W. Ward. *Sensation and Perception.* Orlando. Academic Press, Inc., 1984.
Crouse, William H. *Automotive Mechanics.* New York. McGraw-Hill, 1946.
de Bono, Edward. *New Think.* New York. Avon Books, 1971.
de Bono, Edward. *Po: A Device for Successful Thinking.* New York. Simon and Schuster, 1972.
de Bono, Edward. *Practical Thinking.* New York. Penguin Books, 1979.
de Bono, Edward. *Tactics: The Art and Science of Success.* London. Wm. Collins and Sons Ltd., 1985.
DeLozier, Judith and John Grinder. *Turtles All the Way Down.* Bonny Doon, California. Grinder, DeLozier and Associates, 1987.
Dickens, Charles. *A Christmas Carol, and The Chimes.* New York. Harper and Row, 1965.
Doyle, Arthur Conan. *The Complete Sherlock Holmes.* Garden City, New York. Doubleday and Company, 1930.
Ekman, Paul and Wallace V. Friesen. *Unmasking the Face.* Englewood Cliffs, New Jersey, Prentice-Hall, Inc., 1975.
Ekman, Paul. *Telling Lies.* New York. Norton, 1985.
Electronics Engineering Manual, Volume VII. New York. McGraw-Hill, 1954.

Fabun, Don, ed. *Kaiser Aluminum News.* Vol. 23, No. 3. 1965.
Fast, Julius. *Body Language.* New York. M. Evans, 1970.
Fields, Debbi and Alan Furst. *One Smart Cookie.* New York. Simon and Schuster, 1987.
Gardner, Debbie. *Survive: Don't be a Victim.* New York. Warner Books, 1982.
Gardner, Michael. "Flex Cop." *The VAK Newsletter.* Winter 1986.
Giffin, Kim and Bobby S. Patton. *Fundamentals of Interpersonal Communication.* New York. Harper and Row, 1971.
Gilligan, Stephen G. *Therapeutic Trances: The Cooperative Principle in Ericksonian Hypnotherapy.* New York. Brunner/Mazel, 1987.
Grinder, John and Richard Bandler. *The Structure of Magic, Volume II.* Palo Alto. Science and Behavior Books, 1976.
Grinder, John and Richard Bandler. *Reframing.* Moab, Utah. Real People Press, 1981
Grinder, John and Michael McMaster. *Precision.* Bonny Doon, California. Precision Models, 1980.
Hall, Edward T. *The Dance of Life: The Other Dimension of Time.* Garden City, New York. Anchor Press, 1983.
Hall, Edward T. *The Hidden Dimension.* Garden City, New York. Anchor Books, 1969.
Hall, Edward T. *The Silent Language.* Greenwich, Connecticut. Fawcett, 1959.
Hayakawa, S. I. *Language in Thought and Action.* New York. Harcourt, Brace and World, Inc., 1961.
Heinlein, Robert A. *The Notebooks of Lazarus Long.* G. P. Putnam's Sons, 1978.
Henley, Nancy M. *Body Politics: Power, Sex and Nonverbal Communication.* Englewood Cliffs, New Jersey. Prentice-Hall, 1977.
Henry, Jean M. *Fighting Spirit.* Unpublished manuscript.
Hill, Napoleon and W. Clement Stone. *Success Through a Positive Mental Attitude.* Englewood Cliffs, New Jersey. Prentice-Hall, 1960.
Hingley, Ronald. *The Russian Mind.* New York. Charles Scribner's Sons, 1977.
Houdini, Harry. *Houdini on Magic.* New York. Dover Publications, 1953.
Iacocca, Lee. *Iacocca: An Autobiography.* New York. Bantam, 1984.
Ise, John. *Economics.* New York. Harper, 1950.
Jaynes, Julian. *The Origin of Consciousness in the Breakdown of the Bicameral Mind.* New York. Houghton, Mifflin Co., 1982.
Jordan, Nick. "The Face of Feeling," *Psychology Today.* Vol.2, No. 1, January, 1986.
Knapp, Mark L. *Nonverbal Communication in Human Interaction.* New York. Holt, Rinehart and Winston, 1978.
Korzybski, Alfred. *Science and Sanity: An Introduction to Non-Aristotelian Systems and General Semantics.* Lancaster, Pennsylvania. Science Press Printing Company, 1933.
Laborde, Genie Z. *Influencing with Integrity.* Palo Alto. Syntony, 1983.
LeBoef, Michael. *The Greatest Management Principle in the World.* New York. G. P. Putnam's Sons, 1985.
LeBoef, Michael, *How to Win Customers and Keep Them for Life.* New York, Putnam Publishing Group, 1988.
Lee, Bruce. *The Tao of Jeet Kun Do.* Burbank, California, Ohara Publications, Inc., 1986.
Maltz, Maxwell. *Psycho-Cybernetics.* Hollywood. Wilshire Books, 1967.

Mangino, Bob. "Police Clowns," *Omni.* Vol. 11, No. 1, October 1988.
McKim, Robert H. *Experiences in Visual Thinking.* Monterey, California. Brooks/Cole Publishing Co., 1980.
McLuhan, Marshall. *Understanding Media.* New York. New American Library, 1964.
Molloy John T. *Molloy's Live for Success.* New York. Bantam Books, 1981.
Molloy, John T. *Dress for Success.* New York. Warner Books, 1975.
Morris, Desmond, Peter Collett, Peter Marsh and Marie O'Shaughnessy. *Gestures.* New York. Stein and Day, 1979.
Pace, Roy. *Target Golf.* Tucson. The Body Press, 1986.
Peale, Norman Vincent. *The Power of Positive Thinking.* Englewood Cliffs, New Jersey. Prentice-Hall, 1956.
Richardson, Alan. *Mental Imagery.* New York. Springer Publishing Company, Inc., 1969.
Robson, Mike. *The Journey to Excellence.* Chichester. John Wiley and Sons, 1986.
Rost, H. T. D. *The Golden Rule: A Universal Ethic.* Oxford. George Ronald, 1986.
Russell, Bill and Taylor Branch. *Second Wind: Memoires of an Opiniated Man.* New York. Random House, 1979.
Schiedter, Arnold. "Eying Ways to Improve Performances," *Sports Illustrated,* February 9, 1987.
Simon, Neil. *The Odd Couple.* New York. Random House, 1966.
Siwoff, Seymour. *The Book of Baseball Records.* New York, Seymour Siwoff, 1987.
Sports Illustrated. "Scorecard." August 24, 1987.
Stanislavsky, Konstantin. *Stanislavsky on the Art of the Stage.* New York. Hill and Wang, 1961.
Steiner, Claude. *Games Alcoholics Play.* New York. Grove Press, 1971.
Stevenson, Robert Louis. *Treasure Island.* New York. Charles Scribner's Sons, 1911.
Thayer, Lee. "Communications Systems." Ervin Laszlo, ed., *The Relevance of General Systems Theory.* New York. George Brazillier, 1972.
Thompson, George. *Verbal Judo: Words for Street Survival.* Springfield, Illinois. C. C. Thomas, 1983.
Trisler, Hank. *No Bull Selling.* New York. Frederick Fell, Inc., 1983.
Twain, Mark. *Pudd'nhead Wilson.* New York. Harper and Brothers, 1899.
Wallenchinsky, David. *The Complete Book of the Olympics.* New York. Penguin Books, 1984.
Wang, An. *Lessons: An Autobiography.* Reading, Massachusetts. Addison-Wesley, 1986.
Wells, H. G. "The Truth About Pyecraft," *28 Science Fiction Stories.* New York. Dover Publications, 1952.
Yeager, Jeana, Dick Rutan and Phil Patton. *Voyager.* New York. Alfred A. Knopf, 1987.
Ziglar, Zig. *Zig Ziglar's Secrets of Closing Sales.* New York. Berkley Books, 1984.
Zimbardo, Philip G. *Psychology and Life.* Glenview, Illinois. Scott, Foresman and Company, 1985.

INDEX

Absent Partner Routine, 50, 51
Acknowledge objections, 136, 141, 148, 155, 162
Actions (also see *behavior*), 14, 53, 82, 104
Actors, 97, 98, 111, 113
Adam, 91
Adams, Douglas, 71
Adjusting, 24, 44, 46, 75
Aim, 18
Allen, Woody, 162
and, 138, 141, 148
Andreas, Connirae, 30
Andreas, Steve, 30
Architects, 7, 37, 147
Arguing, 88-89
Arms, 68
Army, U. S., 18, 132
Asner, Ed, 102
Atlanta, 144
Attitude, 6, 71, 99, 105, 109, 131, 139, 152, 154
Bailey, Kenneth E., 140
Bailey, Rodger C., 93
Bandler, Richard, 6, 43, 66, 86, 103, 121
Baron, Bert, 36, 147
Baseball, 10, 18
Basics, 13
Basketball, 18, 41, 97, 115
Beer, Stafford, 6, 134
Behavior, 14, 15, 61, 63, 65, 72, 82, 98, 99
Blacksmith, 144
öBody language,ì 66, 96-98, 107
Boston Pops Orchestra, 104
Brady, David, 119
Breathing, 68, 79, 121, 127, 128, 160
Brock, Lou, 41
Broering, Michael, 5
Buggy whips, 52
Bull's eye, 16, 18
Bunny, Bugs, 134
But, 137, 141, 148, 155
California, 42, 102
Carnegie, Dale, 88
Carrots and sticks, 55
Chan, Charlie, 88
Change, 93, 107
Chemical dependency, 53,
Choices, 24, 25, 52, 89, 91, 92, 101, 104, 105, 141, 162

Christie, Agatha, 65
Cincinnati, 5
Clark, Crawford, 59
Clues to listen for 70-71
Clues to look for, 67-69
Clues, 66, 67, 83
Cobb, Ty, 10
Communicating, 12, 14, 16, 51, 63, 75, 78, 79, 84, 86, 85, 92, 96, 105, 107, 110, 117, 119, 134, 137, 160, 161, 162
Comparing, 72, 73, 75, 76, 131
Computer manuals, 6, 7
Computers, 6
Consequences, 42, 45
Contract Law class, 59
Contrary responses, 90-92
Cool Hand Luke, 13
Crawford Consideration, 59, 120, 161
de Bono, Edward, 57, 88
Decoding, 74
Demonstration, 74, 76
Dickens, Charles, 45
Dictionaries, 14, 100
Dillard, Harrison, 140-141
Dumbo, 109
Edison, Thomas, 133-134
Edwards Air Force Base, 129
Eisenhower, President, 73
Ekman, Paul, 66
Electronic signals, 63
Emerson, Ralph Waldo, 114
Emotional responses, 63, 84
English, 15, 85, 100, 121, 127
Eskimos, 57-58
Ethics, 7, 157-162
Ewing, J. R., 158
Exceptions, 8
Expand your team, 19
Experience, 15, 19, 23, 24, 38, 42, 43, 44, 74, 82, 84, 103, 112, 114, 149, 152
Experiments, 112, 113, 114, 116
Expert, 18, 151
Expressions, 15, 61, 73, 99, 123, 125
Eye contact, 92-93, 99, 107, 116, 117
Eye movements, 93, 100, 124
Eyes, 67
Face, 73
Fagan, Jim, 89

FBI, 99-100, 103
Feel, 23, 31, 37, 38, 39, 41, 43, 44, 45, 46, 50, 56, 63, 64, 75, 124, 148
Feeling, 22, 24, 61
Feelings, 23, 44
Feet, 73
Flint, Captain, 21, 81
Flowers, Frank, 23, 24
Follow the leader, 126, 152
Football, 13, 18, 36, 97
Ford, Henry, 47, 49
Forehead, 67
Frustration, 22, 53
Games, 151-156
Gardner, Debbie, 99, 139
Gardner, Michael, 5, 6, 138, 161
Gestures, 65, 69, 127
Get into it, 19, 41-46, 56
Get on their side, 106, 121, 127-128
Ginsberg, Douglas, 99-100
Gold, 35
Golden Rule, 158, 161
Golf, 33, 84, 109
Grinder, John, 6, 43, 66, 86, 93, 96, 103, 114, 121
Guarantee, 7-8
Habit, 10
Hall, Edward T., 6, 14, 66
Hands, 68
Hawkins, Jim, 21, 22, 81, 82
Hayakawa, S. I., 6
Hayes, Woody, 29
Head, 68
Hear, 23, 31, 37, 38, 39, 41, 43, 44, 45, 46, 50, 63, 64, 75, 120, 124, 148
Hearing, 22, 24, 61, 113
Heinlein, Robert, 54
Henley, Nancy, 105
Hoffman, Tony, 88-89
Holmes, Sherlock, 65, 73, 83
Houdini, Harry, 12
Hungary, 63
Hypothetical situation, 56, 74, 76, 79
Iacocca, Lee, 47, 51, 121
IBM, 55
Ice boxes, 57-58
Indianapolis, 65
Inflection, 71, 125
Information, feeling, 43, 93
Information, hearing, 43, 75, 93, 125

Information, seeing, 43, 75, 93, 125
Intelligence, 133
Intentions, 15, 87, 134
Iran, 51
Jackson, Alan, 93
James, William, 113
Japanese, 121
Jargon, 101, 121, 122
Jaw, 68
Join their team, 49, 58, 59, 60
Jokes, 8, 139, 141
Kangaroo, 31
Kansas City, 29
Kansas, 115, 151
Karate Kid, The, 151
Key clues, 19, 61-76
Key people, 47, 49, 50, 60
Kingsfield, Professor, 59
Klem, Bill, 110
Knapp, Mark L., 6, 66, 71, 92
Korzybski, Alfred, 106
Labels, 96, 106-107
Laborde, Genie Z., 6
Language, feeling, 79, 95, 96, 100, 121
Language, hearing, 95, 96, 100, 121
Language, seeing, 79, 95, 96, 100, 121
Languages, 121, 122
Laser, 36
Lateral thinking, 57
Laurel and Hardy, 102
Law of Supply and Demand, 58
LeBoef, Michael, 26, 54
Lee, Bruce, 133
Lemberkovits, Antonius, 63
Listen to them, 122, 128
Listen, 145, 76
Livesy, Dr. 21, 22, 81
Locksmith, 133
Look the part, 121, 123
Look, 42, 76, 144, 145
Lower body, 68
Macy's, 88
Madison, Oscar, 95
Maltz, Maxwell, 114
Manipulation, 7, 149, 157-162
Manning, Danny, 115
Map, 21, 22, 81
Martin, Strother, 13
Mason, Mark, 36, 147
Master keys, 12
Matching, 121, 123-128, 152-153, 156

McKim, Robert H., 6, 41, 45
McLuhan, Marshall, 86

Meaning, 15, 65, 66, 71, 85, 86, 87, 99, 101
Medley, Marilyn, 24
Memory, 22, 23
Mental images, 23, 27, 31, 38, 43, 44, 46, 50, 95, 101, 114, 116
Mental rehearsal, 41-42, 78, 111, 114, 117
Menu, 25, 26, 27
Merger, Martin, 90
Messages, 15, 16, 50, 66, 74, 83, 85, 87, 98, 134, 141
Messages, nonverbal, 14, 15, 16, 56, 96, 98, 99, 104, 120, 149, 152, 154
Messages verbal, 79, 98, 104
Misinterpreting, 66, 83
Molloy, John T., 92, 98
Money, 14, 49, 54
Mood, 75, 76, 71, 73, 129-131, 152, 154
Motrine, Monica, 25
Mouth, 68
Movements, 83, 121, 123, 126, 128, 153
Mrs. Fields' Cookies, 58
Mundy, Phil, 56-57
Mutual benefit, 49, 59, 134, 157, 159
Mutual trust, 59, 79, 100, 103, 105, 118-128, 134, 148
Narrow the field, 50
National Football League, 13
Nicklaus, Jack, 41
Objections, 79, 136-141
Obvious, 8, 22, 57, 83
Oklahoma, 115
Olsen, Dolores, 54-55
Olympics, 18, 63
Oregon, 140
Other words, 138, 141, 156
Pace, Roy, 33
Patterns, 53, 72, 73, 82, 84, 103, 127, 133, 153
Patterns, interrupting, 138-139, 141
Pause, 13, 124
Pcale, Norman Vincent, 30
Performance anxiety, 112
Pet words and phrases, 79, 101, 121, 127, 128
Pictures, mental, 23, 24

Pitch, 71, 79, 125, 154
Police, 5, 96, 138
Posture, 69, 79, 83, 99, 105, 121, 123, 126, 128, 153, 160, 162
Pressure, 109
Process, 14, 24, 63
Prospectors, 35
Pyecraft, 29
Qualify, 49, 51, 57, 71
Questions, 37, 38, 39, 56, 103, 121, 122, 154
Radar, 61, 63, 65, 72, 154
Radio, 24, 63
Random Air Lines, 9
Random way, the, 10, 11, 22, 29
Rate of speech, 71, 79, 125, 153
Reagan, Ronald, 106
Receiving messages, 12-13
Reeder, Ella, 105
Refining, 19, 24, 32, 36, 37, 39, 44, 55
Refrigerator, 24-25
Rehearsal, 115
Religion, 14, 158
Resourceful attitude, 59, 78, 79, 99, 109-117, 134, 148, 162
Result, negative, 29
Result, positive, 19, 29, 30, 32, 33
Results you want, 5, 7, 8, 10, 13, 16, 19, 22, 27, 35, 38, 42, 45, 78, 79, 148, 151, 158
Results, improving, 14
Results, specific, 11
Results, to get, 5, 10, 14, 78, 79
Rhythm, 71
Rooney, Andy, 94
Ropes course, 113-114
Roses, 23. 24
Russell, Bill, 43, 66
Rutan, Burt, 129-131
Rutan, Dick, 129-131
Safety, 18, 83
Salina, 144
Samaritan, The Good, 140
San Francisco, 35, 140, 144
Scrooge, Ebenezer, 45
See, 23, 31, 37, 38, 39, 44, 45, 46, 50, 63, 64, 75, 120, 124, 148
Seed, 26-27
Seeing, 22, 24, 61, 113
Self-defense, 7, 99, 139, 149, 159
Self-image, 110
Sellers, Bob, 50
Sending messages, 12-13

Senses, 22, 24, 42, 61, 63
Sessions, William, 100
Show and Tell Chart, 100, 124
Sights, 24
Signals, (also see *messages*) 16, 19, 46, 66, 61, 63, 64, 73, 75, 99, 131, 136, 143, 144
Signals, coded, 64
Signals, nonverbal, 59, 61, 64, 66, 79, 83
Signs, (also see *messages* and *signals*) 44, 126
Silence, 13
Silver, Long John, 81
Smell, 23, 41, 43, 63
Smelling, 22, 61
Smoky Mountains, 56-57
Sounds, 24, 42, 144
Sounds, mental, 23
Space program, 115
Spanish, 95, 121
Speak their language, 121, 128
Specific words, 101
Stage fright, 112
Steps, 8, 16, 22, 78, 79, 120, 147
Stevenson, Robert Louis, 21
Stewart, Ross, 93
Stone, W. Clement, 30
Stories, 79, 139-140, 141
Studio of your mind, 43
Superstition, 103-104
Surprise, 79, 138, 141, 161
Swift, Johathan, 88
Symbols, 14, 23
Target way, the, 11
Target, clear, 36, 37, 78, 99, 160, 162
Target, positive, 30, 32, 33, 42, 55
Target, specific, 85
Target, thinking of, 20-27
Targets, recognizing, 143-145
Targets, testing, 42, 46, 148
Targets, two with one shot, 57, 58
Tasting, 22, 61, 63
Technical language, 101
Telephone, 128
The Odd Couple, 95
Thinking, 19
Thinking, nonverbal, 23
Thinking, verbal, 23
Thompson, George J., 97
Tisler, Hank, 117, 122
Tools, 7, 106, 159

Traps, 6, 7, 59, 66, 78, 80-107, 121, 134, 148, 160
Treasure Island, 21, 81
Treasure, 21
Treat, Jim, 144
Trelawney, Squire, 21, 22, 81
Trust, 53, 79, 122, 123, 125, 128, 139, 160
Turn signals, 56
Twain, Mark, 91
Unger, Felix, 95
USA, 85
Use your clues, 129-132, 134, 144, 160
USSR, 85
Values, 161
Victim, 99
Visual clues, 72, 75, 76
Visualization, 41-42, 114
Vocal clues, 72, 75, 76
Voice, 73, 121, 123, 125, 127, 128, 162
Volume, 71, 79, 125
Voyager, 129
Waetjen, Ray, 140
Wang, An, 81-82
Warm or cool, 61, 63, 75, 79, 131, 148
Washington, D. C., 56-57, 89
Watson, Dr., 73
Watson, John, 71
Wells, H. G., 29
Wichita, 144
Words, 14, 15, 16, 23, 27, 44, 53, 65, 71, 83, 93, 94, 98, 100, 103, 104, 110, 121, 127, 138
Words, feel, 103, 156
Words, hear, 103, 156
Words, see, 103, 156y
Working smart, 7
Yeager, Jeana, 129
Zero, 18
Ziglar, Zig, 97, 98